Saint Joseph Sisters of

Constitutions of the Congregation of the Sisters of St. Joseph

Saint Joseph Sisters of

Constitutions of the Congregation of the Sisters of St. Joseph

ISBN/EAN: 9783337733391

Printed in Europe, USA, Canada, Australia, Japan

Cover: Foto ©ninafisch / pixelio.de

More available books at **www.hansebooks.com**

CONSTITUTIONS

OF THE

CONGREGATION

OF THE

SISTERS OF ST. JOSEPH.

NEW YORK
O'SHEA & CO.

APPROBATION.

FRANCIS PAUL DE NEUVILLE DE VILLEROY, by the mercy of God and authority of the Holy See, Archbishop and Count of Lyons, Primate of France, Commander of the Royal Orders, having examined the book entitled Constitutions of the little Congregation of the Sisters of Saint Joseph, established at Lyons; and having found nothing but what is most edifying and conformable to Christian charity, we have permitted and permit, by these presents, that it be printed and distributed in our diocese.

Given at Lyons, the 20th December, 1729.

(Signed.)
ANTHONY,
Bishop of Synope, Suffragan of **Lyons,**
Vicar **General.**

CHARIZIEU, *Secretary.*

PREFACE.

The Congregation of the Sisters **of Saint Joseph** originated in France, in the **town of Puy, in** Velay, where Bishop **Henry de Maupas established** it, at the suggestion **of** Father **John** Peter Médaille, a celebrated **missioner of** the Society of Jesus.

This zealous missioner having found, **in the** course of his missions, several young women who desired to retire from the world, and manifested at the same time very great dispositions for works of piety, and especially for the good of their neighbor, formed the project of proposing to some Bishop **to establish** a congregation of pious women.

Accordingly, he addressed himself **to the** Bishop of Puy, Henry de Maupas; being convinced, from the knowledge he had of the sublime virtue and extraordinary zeal of this **great prelate** for the glory of God and the salvation of his neighbor, that he would not reject the proposition.

The Bishop at once approved of the proposal, and invited those pious souls to assemble at Puy, and there make their first establishment.

During some months after their arrival at Puy, they lodged at the house of a pious lady, who not only contributed to the utmost of her power to the formation of the establishment, but moreover labored with an extraordinary zeal and charity for their advancement till her death.

All things being arranged by the Bishop for the execution of so pious a design, he placed under their care the Asylum for Female Orphans, at Puy. On the 15th of October, 1650, the Feast of St. Teresa, he addressed them in a pathetic discourse, animating them to the most pure love of God, and to a most perfect charity towards their neighbor. He afterwards placed them under the protection of the glorious St. Joseph, and ordered that they should be called the *Congregation of the Sisters of St. Joseph.* He gave them rules for their guidance, and prescribed for them a form of dress; finally, he confirmed the establishment of the same Congregation and the prescribed rules, by letters of the 10th of March, 1651; and, during his life, manifested great zeal for the success of the Congregation, many establishments of which he erected in his own diocese.

After his death his successor, Bishop Armant de Betune, convinced by experience of the great services the Sisters had rendered to God and to their neighbor, in his diocese, confirmed the Congregation and the rules observed by the Sisters since their establishment, by letters of the 23d September, 1665.

Louis XIV. confirmed by letters patent the first establishment of the Sisters of this Congregation in the cities of Puy, St. Didier, and in several other places of Velay.

Since that time, Almighty God has so graciously protected this Congregation, that, by His grace, it has been introduced into the dioceses of Clermont, Vienne, Lyons, Grenoble, Embrun, Gap, Sisteron, Vivier, Uzes, and several others.

This Congregation is at present introduced into almost all the dioceses of France. It also has establishments in Savoy and Corsica. In the year 1836, six Sisters of the Congregation arrived at St. Louis, State of Missouri, America, under the auspices of the much revered Bishop of that diocese, Joseph Rosati. The first house established by them is that at Carondolet, a small village, five miles distant from St. Louis. This house was made the Novitiate of the Congregation in the year 1844, and from it houses have been established in nearly all the cities of the West.

In 1847, Rt. Rev. Bp. Kenrick petitioned the Rt. Rev. Bishop of St. Louis for some Sisters of St. Joseph to take charge of St. John's Orphan Asylum in Philadelphia. The request was most readily granted, and Mother St. John (Fournier) with several Sisters, took charge of that institution. There are at present (1884) sixteen houses in the diocese of Philadelphia ; three in Maryland, and four in New Jersey, subject to the Mother House at Chestnut Hill, Philadelphia.

In 1851 a Foundation of Sisters, in charge of Mother Delphine, was sent from Chestnut Hill to Toronto, C. W.

In September, 1856, a Foundation of Sisters was sent from Chestnut Hill to the diocese of Brooklyn, at the invitation of Rt. Rev. Bp. Loughlin, D. D. There are now (1884) eighteen mission houses of the Sisters of St. Joseph in the Brooklyn diocese.

In 1866 the Sisters of St. Joseph were introduced into the diocese of St. Augustine in the State of Florida by the saintly Bishop Verot. On the 27th of July of that year eight Sisters left Le Puy for America and arrived in the city of St. Augustine on the 2nd of September. In 1880 a regular Novitiate was established under the auspices of Bishop Moore. There are now (1884) six communities of this Congregation in the diocese, viz.: at St. Augustine, Jacksonville, Fernandina, Palatka, Mandarin, and St. Ambrose in St. Johns Co.

It has been found necessary to print the Constitutions of the Congregation, which have been translated from the French edition of Lyons, 1827, given to the public by order of the Most Reverend Jean Paul Gaston de Pins, Archbishop of Amisia, and Apostolic Administrator of the diocese of Lyons.

INDEX.

Preface and Approbation of the Congregation, 1

PART I.

Constitutions of the Congregation of the Sisters of St. Joseph. 2
Chapter I.—Of the Origin and Name of this Congregation. 3
Chapter II.—Of the Vows made in the Congregation 4
Chapter III.—Of the Enclosure of the Sisters, 6.
Chapter IV.—Of the Dress of the Sisters, . 7
Chapter V.—Of the Office, and Prayers of the Sisters, ... 8
Chapter VI.—Of the Superiors of the Congregation, ... 9
Chapter VII.—Of the Spiritual Father, . . 10
Chapter VIII.—Of the Associated Sisters, . 12
Chapter IX.—Of Humility, and of the Rank of the Sisters, ... 16

PART II.

Chapter I.—The End of the Congregation, . 18
Chapter II.—The Means of Perfection of the Sisters, ... 19
Chapter III.—Of the Duties the Sisters owe to their Neighbor, ... 21
Chapter IV.—Of the Charity of the Sisters towards one another, ... 25
Chapter V.—Of the Care of Sick and Dying Sisters, ... 28
Chapter VI.—Of Charity towards Deceased Sisters, ...

PART III.

Chapter I.—Of the Reception of Novices, . 32
Chapter II.—Of the Qualities required in them, 35
Chapter III.—Of the Novitiate and Education of Novices. 37
Chapter IV.—Of the Profession and of the Vows of the Sisters, ... 40
Chapter V.—Of the Vow of Obedience, . . 42
Chapter VI.—Of the Vow of Chastity, . . 45
Chapter VII.—Of the Vow of Poverty, . . 47

PART IV.

Chapter I.—Rules for the Superior, . . 52
Chapter II.—Rules for the Assistant, . . 58
Chapter III.—Rules for the Coadjutrix and Mistress of Novices, ... 60
Chapter IV.—Rules for the Procuratrix, . . 64
Chapter V.—Rules for the Monitor, . . 68
Chapter VI.—Rules for the Counsellors, . . 69
Chapter VII.—Rules for the Attendant on the Poor, ... 71
Chapter VIII.—Rules for the Conductress of Mercy, ... 73
Chapter IX.—Rules for the Portress, . . 75
Chapter X.—Rules for the other officers, . 77
Chapter XI.—Of the Appointment of officers, 78
Chapter XII.—Of the Election of the Superior, 79
Chapter XIII.—Of the Rules applicable to all the Sisters, ... 85
Directions for Sisters Employed in the Schools 90
Chapter I.—Of the Directress of the School, . 90
Chapter II.—Rules for the Sister Teacher, . 92

PART V.

Of the Spiritual Exercises to be Practised by the Sisters, ... 94
Chapter I.—Of the Annual Exercises, . . 94
Chapter II.—Of the Exercises of each Month, 97
Chapter III.—Of the Exercises of each Week, 98

	PAGE
Chapter IV.—Of the Exercises of each Day,	99
Chapter V.—Of the Distribution of the Time of the Day, or the Orarium,	100

PART VI.

Of the Means of Advancing and Sustaining the Congregation,	104
Chapter I.—Of the Means of Receiving none but good Subjects into the Congregation,	104
Chapter II.—Of the means of Destroying Ambition,	105
Chapter III.—Of Avoiding a bad Choice of Superiors,	107
Chapter IV.—Of the Means of Preventing Superiors Abusing their Authority,	108
Chapter V.—Of the Means of Preventing Negligence on the part of the Superior,	109
Chapter VI.—Of Conferences,	111
Chapter VII.—Of the Chapter of Faults,	112
Chapter VIII.—Of Avoiding either Deficiency or Excess in Temporal Goods,	116
Chapter IX.—Of Avoiding Idleness and Disunion,	117
Chapter X.—Of Avoiding too much intercourse with Lay persons,	119
Chapter XI.—Of Avoiding Many Directors,	121
Chapter XII.—Of Avoiding all Restraint in matters of Conscience,	121
Chapter XIII.—Of the Obligation of Knowing and Keeping the Constitutions,	123
Maxims of Perfection,	127

DIRECTORY

FOR THE SISTERS OF ST. JOSEPH.

PART I.

Of the Daily Exercises,	145
Chapter I.—Of rising in the Morning,	145

Chapter II—Of the Meditation, . . . 148
Chapter III.—Of the Office, and Vocal Prayer, 153
Chapter IV.—Of the Mass, ... 155
Chapter V.—Of Work and Silence, . . 160
Chapter VI.—Of Meals, ... 161
Chapter VII.—Of Recreation, . . . 162
Chapter VIII.—Of Morning and Evening Examination of Conscience, ... 164
Chapter IX.—On Going to Bed. . . . 166

PART II.

Exercises of the Week, ... 168
Chapter I.—Manner of Sanctifying all the Days of the week, ... 168
Chapter II.—Of Confession, ... 170
Chapter III.—Of Holy Communion, . . 173
Chapter IV.—Of Fasting. Discipline and other Practices of the Week, ... 177

PART III.

Exercises of each Month, ... 178
Chapter I.—Of the Protestations, . . . 178
Chapter II.—Of the Patrons of each month, and other Exercises, ... 181

PART IV.

Annual Exercises. 182
Chapter I.—The Manner of Beginning the Year, 182
Chapter II.—Of Retreats and Annual Renovation of Vows, ... 184
Manner of Receiving and Giving the Habit to the Sisters of St. Joseph, . . . 186
Form of the Act to be Written on the Reception of Sisters, ... 194
Form of the Act to be Written for a Profession, 192
Letter of Bishop Henry de Maupas, of Puy, for the Establishment of the Sisters of St. Joseph, 195
The original Memorial presented to the Holy Father, on the Canonization of the Japanese Martyrs, ... 198
Response of the Holy Father, . . . 199

CONSTITUTIONS

OF THE

CONGREGATION OF THE SISTERS

OF

SAINT JOSEPH.

These Constitutions are divided into Six Parts.

Part I.—Explains the nature of this Congregation.

Part II.—Treats of the object for which it was instituted.

Part III.—Enumerates the qualities required in those who desire to be received into it.

Part IV.—Contains the special rules for the Superiors, and the general rules for all the Sisters.

Part V.—Treats of the spiritual exercises which the Sisters are to practise.

Part VI.—Points out the proper means for preserving and advancing this Congregation.

Each Part is divided into Chapters, in which all that is contained in the Constitutions is explained in due order.

CONSTITUTIONS.

PART I.

Of the Nature of the Congregation of Saint Joseph.

CHAPTER I.

OF THE ORIGIN AND NAME OF THIS CONGREGATION.

This Congregation, according to the design with which God inspired its Founder, consists of an association of pious females, who have freely chosen to live in community, for the purpose of applying themselves to the attainment of Christian perfection and the service of their neighbor, by observing the rules which are prescribed in the following Constitutions.

It is called the Congregation of Saint Joseph, because, in imitation of their glorious Patron, its members should serve their neighbor with the same care, diligence, charity and love with which this glorious Patriarch served his reputed Son, Jesus Christ, and the Blessed Virgin Mary, his most pure spouse. It is consecrated to the Most Blessed Trinity—Father, Son, and Holy Ghost—under the protection of Mary and Joseph. Hence the Sisters ought, in imitation of Mary and Joseph, incessantly to glorify the Most Holy Trinity by the practice of all the virtues, but especially by a most profound humility.

The Sisters shall endeavor, in their entire conduct, to emulate the spirit of the Sisters of the Visitation, Founded by Saint Francis de Sales; they shall always entertain the most sincere veneration for the founder of that religious order, and shall do all in their power to adopt the spirit with which he inspired that order in its institution.

CHAPTER II.

OF THE VOWS WHICH ARE MADE IN THE CONGREGATION.

After two years of novitiate, the Sisters shall make the three simple vows of poverty, chastity, and obedience, together with a protestation of practising, in everything and on all occasions, the most profound humility, and the most cordial charity and kindness towards all persons.

They shall be bound to keep perpetually

these three simple vows, with as much fidelity and exactness as if they were solemn; and they cannot be dispensed from them as long as they are in the Congregation. But if they leave it, or be dismissed from it, the Bishop of the place in which they are at the time of quitting the Congregation, may dispense them from the three vows. This dispensation should be given in writing. Should any Sister seek to be expelled and to be dispensed from her vows, she would be guilty of a most grievous sin, of which she must repent in order to save her soul. The Bishop, however, has the power of dispensing in all such cases; and can lawfully exercise it for the advantage of the Congregation. Such dispensations are not to be granted; unless after mature, patient and charitable consideration of the case, and after all other means of remedying the evil arising from fickle or incorrigible subjects, shall have been employed. Should any Sister clandestinely leave the Congregation, those interested in her welfare, and the honor of religion, should procure her return, either to the house she left, or to some other house of the Congregation, where she shall remain for some days, during which proper means shall be employed to bring her to a sense of duty, by adopting charitable remonstrances, and should she remain in her spirit of insubordination, the Bishop will dispense her from her vows, and send her to her friends.

Should such Sisters have brought with them any property, real or personal, the Superiors who received such property, must return it to them, without interest, except the furniture, clothes, and linen which have deteriorated by use. And should it appear that they have worn out more than they brought with them into the Congregation, the Superiors will not then be obliged to give them anything, except as far as Christian charity may inspire them.

When the Sisters leave the Congregation, the Crucifix and habit should be taken from them, and orders given them, not to wear such things when they go home.

CHAPTER III.

OF THE ENCLOSURE OF THE SISTERS.

The Sisters do not observe a strict enclosure; because according to their Institute, they devote themselves to the service of their neighbor, and to visit the sick both at home and abroad; they should, however, avoid all useless visits, and should never go out, without the permission of their Superiors.

There shall be, if possible, in each house, a dormitory, partitioned into bedrooms, each Sister having a small room and bed; and if each Sister cannot have a separate room, it is necesary that each one have her own bed; and that—even in case of sickness—

no person ever enter the sleeping apartment without the permission of the Superior.

If circumstances permit, there shall be an apartment to receive any ladies desirous of making a spiritual retreat: and rooms also may be set apart for conversing on matters of charity. The Sisters who may be established in hospitals, or in orphan asylums, or in Magdalen houses, shall, as far as possible, conform to the above directions, but in every case an apartment should be alloted to them for sleeping, or for their devotions and other exercises, to which lay persons should not have access, without the leave of the Superior.

CHAPTER IV.

OF THE DRESS OF THE SISTERS.

The habit of the Sisters shall resemble the dress of humble widows, made of common woolen stuff, of a black color. The body of the dress is to be perfectly plain, as also the sleeves, which shall extend to the end of the hand. The skirts of their habits are not to reach quite to the ground; their shoes are to be black and plain.

The Sisters shall wear a band of white linen across the forehead; also a plain white linen cap fastened under the chin, another cap of black woolen stuff with a veil of the same material. They shall wear a crucifix of brass attached to the neck, which shall hang before the breast. They shall wear a pair of black beads attached to the left side of their cincture or cord.

The servants of the Sisters shall dress in the same manner, except that the materials of their dress shall be coarser, and they shall wear a cap of black taffeta, without veil or band.

The Sisters shall not take off their dress during the day, either on account of their work, or of the heat of the day. In sickness they can use a dressing gown, which shall be of the same material as their usual habit.

CHAPTER V.

OF THE OFFICE AND PRAYERS OF THE SISTERS.

In order that the Sisters may be free to employ themselves in the service of their neighbor, they shall not be bound either to say or to sing the Divine Office, in choir or in private; consequently, they shall not be obliged to learn either plain chant or music, not only because these acquirements are unnecessary for their state, but would expose them to loss of time, and be a source of distraction. Those, however, who have a Chapel in their house, are allowed to sing the Vespers of the Blessed Virgin, on Sundays and Festivals, at two o'clock in the afternoon; and those Sisters in Hospitals can also sing

Vespers on the same days in the Hospital Chapel.

The Sisters in the Orphan Asylums, or Magdalen Asylums, can train their inmates to sing the Office alternately with themselves. The Sisters who have no Chapel shall assist at Vespers in the Parish Church.

Though the Sisters be not bound to choir-duties, or to the Divine Office, they have every day, hours for prayer and other exercises of devotion, which will be prescribed in the fifth part of these constitutions.

CHAPTER VI.

OF THE SUPERIORS OF THE CONGREGATION.

The Sisters of the Congregation shall consider the Bishops of the respective dioceses in which they reside as their Superiors; they shall show them profound respect, submission, and obedience in all things which they may prescribe, considering them as holding the place of Jesus Christ, and invested with his authority over them.

The Bishops can visit the houses of this community, established in their respective dioceses, and demand an account of both the temporal and spiritual state of their houses; they can examine, correct, and even punish, according as prudence and charity may suggest to them.

They can make regulations for their general good; and for the maintenance and execution of the present Constitutions.

They can also, if they deem it useful or necessary, change Superiors and Sisters from one house to another, and even send them to other dioceses, where they are demanded, or for other purposes consistent with the object of this Community.

When any Superiors or other Sisters in office, desire to renounce their charge, or when it is found necessary to depose them, the Bishops can do so, and name others in their places.

The Bishops are most humbly requested to have for this Congregation a paternal charity, and special care for its maintenance and advancement, in consideration of the great Saint Francis de Sales, whose spirit and views, in the institution of the religious of the Visitation, it is the object of this Congregation to perpetuate.

CHAPTER VII.

OF THE SPIRITUAL FATHER.

As the Bishops are frequently occupied entirely in the affairs of their dioceses, or live at a distance from the houses of the Sisters, and hence are unable to attend the wants of this Congregation, they can, therefore, name one or more Spiritual Fathers, according to the number and distance of the houses established in their respective dioceses. It would be desirable, that these Spiritual Fathers were not at too great distances, that so they might watch over the houses, and that the Sisters might have recourse to them, when their counsel and authority should be required.

The Bishops will be pleased to choose for this office secular or regular priests, distinguished for their charity, prudence and probity; and the Sisters also may suggest to the Bishop any persons. whom they deem suitable for the purpose.

The Spiritual Fathers shall possess the right of Vicars-General of the Bishops, over all the houses committed to their care.

Each Spiritual Father shall visit once a year, all the houses under his jurisdiction, in company with the Confessors of the Sisters, or with some other prudent ecclesiastic; and, in his presence, shall interrogate each Sister, one after another, and having listened with patience to all that they may have to say respecting the welfare of their house or Congregation, he will then assemble them all in Chapter, when he will make such corrections or give such instructions as he shall deem proper for the reformation and perfection of the Community.

He shall examine the accounts presented by the Superior of the receipts and expenditures, since the last visit. If he find them correct, he shall approve them and sign them; if otherwise, he shall note the error, and also sign it. He shall also make such regulations as he may deem necessary for the reformation and welfare of the house; provided they be not contrary to those made by the Bishop, or to the Constitutions.

He shall accompany the Bishop in his visits to the Sisters; and in the absence of the Bishop, he shall preside at the election of Superiors; he shall see that the rules be strictly observed, that no abuse, change, nor relaxation of the rules, be introduced among the Sisters; and in case of any infraction of rules, he shall correct them, and impose such penances on those guilty of them as he may deem suitable; having first consulted with the Superior. He cannot, however, depose Superiors, without the order of the Bishop.

The Sisters may have recourse to the Spiritual Father in all important cases, temporal or spiritual; and having conferred with him, whatever he, with the council of the Superior and her advisers, shall have decided on, shall be punctually executed. If any difficulty occur which cannot be decided, it shall be referred to the Bishop.

CHAPTER VIII.

OF THE ASSOCIATED SISTERS.

As there are a great many young persons

called by God to a holy and retired life, in places where there exist no establishment of the Sisterhood, the Sisters of St. Joseph can, with the permission of the Bishop, and advice of the Spiritual Father, enroll in their Congregation such persons, and establish small communities of three or four of them in the places of their residence, and such persons so enrolled shall be called "Associated Sisters."

The Bishops and the Spiritual Fathers shall be their Superiors. They shall depend on the house of the Congregation which has enrolled them, and which shall watch over them and their conduct; it shall correct them and give information about them, if necessary, to the Spiritual Father, who shall visit them at least once a year, as the other Sisters.

The Associated Sisters shall dress in the same manner as the Sisters of the Congregation, with this exception, that they shall wear a plain white linen cap, and the crucifix which they shall have suspended from their neck is to be smaller than that of the Sisters of the Congregation.

Before they take the habit of Associated Sisters, they shall remain for at least three months in the house of the Associated Sisters, in order to be tried, after which the Superior of the principal house shall examine them, or shall appoint some Sister to do so, at which examination the Spiritual Father shall be present, if be it deemed necessary. If considered suitable, they shall receive the habit of Associated Sisters from the Superior in the oratory or chapel of their residence.

Having taken the habit, they shall perform two years of novitiate, at the termination of which they shall be examined in the same manner as before the reception of the habit. If not deemed capable of making their profession, they shall be rejected; but if judged suitable, they shall make their profession, by taking the three simple vows of poverty, chastity, and obedience, as long as they remain among the Associated Sisters: so that if they should leave of their own accord, or if they should be expelled for any considerable fault, they would be entirely free from their vows, without any other dispensation.

They shall observe, as far as possible, all the rules prescribed in these Constitutions, excepting that they shall ordinarily receive the Holy Communion only on the great Festivals and Sundays, and even then not without the permission of their Confessor and of their Superior. Neither are they obliged to say the Offices of the Holy Ghost, or of the Blessed Virgin, or the Litanies of Jesus, of Mary, of St. Joseph, or of All Saints. If, however, they have time, and desire to say them, they can do so.

One of the Associates shall be appointed to read the subject of meditation, the spiritual lectures, and also, occasionally, a chapter of the Constitutions, to the end that these may be well understood and punctually observed.

There is to be no Assistant, but in case of the absence of the Superior, the senior Sister shall hold the first rank, and shall govern the house. If any scandal occur in the house of the Associated Sisters, the Superior of the house shall promptly correct it, by charitably admonishing the guilty. If this does not suffice, she shall inform the Spiritual Father, in order that he may remedy the matter, and inflict suitable penances, or cause a change to another house, if he should judge this more advisable. If these means prove ineffectual, the guilty shall be dismissed from the house, and the crosses and habits shall be taken from them. Whatever they brought with them, unless consumed by use, shall be returned to them, without any interest thereon. They shall then be considered as freed from their vows, which were only taken for as long as they might continue associated to the Community.

Should it happen, which may God forbid, that all the Sisters of any Community should misconduct themselves, or give any grievous scandal, in case the evil is beyond all remedy, the Community shall be dissolved, the crosses and habits shall be taken from them, and they shall return to their respective homes.

CHAPTER IX.

OF HUMILITY, AND OF THE RANK OF THE SISTERS.

As humility is the foundation of all virtue, the character of the true disciples of Jesus Christ, and the firm support of the entire edifice of religious perfection,—the Sisters shall accordingly, from their very entrance into the Congregation, labor incessantly for its acquisition, by asking it of Almighty God, and by practising it both exteriorly and interiorly on every occasion.

They will practise this virtue interiorly, by entertaining humble and lowly sentiments of themselves; by despising themselves; by considering the number of their sins, their extreme weakness, their utter misery. Nor is it sufficient that the mind be convinced of all this; the heart must also embrace these truths. The truly humble love to be humbled, to be despised by every one, to suffer humiliations, contempt and opposition.

They will practise this virtue exteriorly, in seeking after, or at least in receiving with courage, the most lowly employments, the most painful offices, and in showing a perfect sweetness of temper in their conversations; in submitting freely to the opinions and guidance of others, in manifesting an unfeigned esteem and condescension to one another, as persons consecrated to God, and true spouses to Jesus Christ. The younger Sisters should be most respectful both to their Superiors and to their seniors; and to all their elders, though newly admitted into the Community. All should manifest great respect towards persons of the world, and on no account to despise any one, however poor or miserable.

In order to preserve good order in the Congregation, and lest indiscretion in the exercise of humility should introduce confusion amongst the Sisters, it is required that the Superiors in every house hold the first place; and the Assistant Superior shall hold the second place.—As to the remaining Sisters, whatever may be the office they fill in the house, they shall always rank according to their seniority in the Community; so that without considering either age, or merit, those that have been professed the first, shall always take the precedence.

Hence, if any Superior of a house, travelling through obedience, should arrive in any other house of the Congregation, the Superior of the house where she is arrived shall invariably place her in the third place, giving her the place next to the Assistant, because it is fitting to honor those of the Congregation who bear the name of Superior.

PART II.

Of the End of the Establishment of the Sisters of Saint Joseph, and of the Means of arriving at it.

CHAPTER I.

THE END OF THIS CONGREGATION.

This Congregation was established in order to associate, in one body, those persons who, though not called to a life of strict enclosure, nevertheless desire to quit the world, to aspire to perfection, and to assist their neighbor in all spiritual and temporal necessities. Hence this Congregation is established for two principal ends.

The first is, that the persons admitted to it, labor incessantly for their own sanctification by the practise of every virtue, and that they aspire to the most sublime perfection.

The second is, that the neighbor be assisted by every work of mercy, both spiritual and corporal, that may be in the power of the Sisters of the Congregation. We shall lay down in the following chapters the means of attaining these ends.

CHAPTER II.

THE MEANS TO BE ADOPTED BY THE SISTERS FOR ACQUIRING PERFECTION.

To acquire the perfection which God demands of the members of this Congregation, they must, in the first place, observe faithfully the vows they have made, and all the rules prescribed in these Constitutions. Hence they should frequently read them with attention, and with an earnest desire of keeping them all, even the smallest.

Besides these general means, there are other special ones which they shall adopt, and which will be most advantageous towards advancing them in perfection. They should often repeat these words of the Sacred Scripture: "*Be ye holy as I am holy;*" and these others pronounced by Jesus Christ to his disciples: "*Be ye perfect as your Father in Heaven is perfect.*" They should consider these as addressed to themselves; and in obedience to the voice of the Eternal Father, and of His Divine Son, they should conceive an ardent desire of becoming holy and perfect, by the practise of every virtue. They should especially labor to acquire humility, which is the foundation of all sanctity, and charity, which is true perfection. But as all virtues are the pure gift of God, they should ask them of the Divine Bounty, every day with great earnestness and perseverance, and endeavor to practise them on every occasion that may present itself. They should also remember that this Congregation is consecrated to the most Adorable Trinity, Father, Son, and Holy Ghost, and to the Blessed Virgin and Saint Joseph. The Sisters should, then, in all things, try to aspire to what is most perfect, in honor of the Eternal Father, the model of their perfection; they should study to be truly humble and to be despised by all, in imitation of the Son, who, though God from all eternity, came in the likeness of a sinner and says to us: "*Learn of me because I am humble of heart;*" and in honor of the Holy Ghost, the substantial love of the Father and Son, they should in all their actions be animated by the most pure love of God.

To honor Jesus Christ who burned with zeal for the glory of His Father, and for the salvation of mankind, they should be inflamed with similar zeal to maintain and advance, as far as may be in their power, the greater glory of God, and the salvation of their neighbor. In honor of the glorious Virgin Mary, who received the plenitude of the graces of the Holy Ghost, they should be faithful to all the graces they receive from God, and be influenced in all their actions by the inspirations of the Holy Ghost, and not by mere inclination or whim. In honor of **their glorious Patriarch, Saint Joseph, who en-**

tertained for Jesus and Mary the most perfect charity, the Sisters should live with one another in the most perfect union and unalterable friendship, assisting one another with affection, bearing one another's faults with all sweetness; and apply themselves on all occasions to the exercises of charity and works of mercy towards their neighbor. To attain the perfection of which the Sisters of this Congregation make profession, they should imitate, as far as possible, with God's grace, the life of Jesus, Mary and Joseph, by the faithful practise of all virtues, in becoming like to them, so that it may no longer be said that it is they who live, but that it is Jesus who liveth in them, as he lived in Mary and Joseph. To this happy state they will, with God's grace, assuredly arrive, if they punctually correspond with its inspirations, and faithfully employ all the means their holy state affords them, for this purpose.

CHAPTER III.

OF THE DUTIES WHICH THE SISTERS **OUGHT** TO RENDER TO THEIR NEIGHBOR.

Jesus Christ did not come into this world alone to glorify His Father by His adoration, and by a life of the most eminent sanctity and perfection; but, as the Apostle St. Paul informs us, He took the form of a servant in order that He might serve men. This infinite charity induced Him to shed the last drop of His blood, and sacrifice His life to deliver them from the temporal and eternal miseries to which they were exposed.

In imitation of this divine model, the Sisters should not content themselves with their own perfection; but ought to consecrate themselves to the service of their neighbor, if they aspire to attain the whole end of their holy institute.

Hence they undertake in general all the duties of charity and works of mercy; they serve the poor in hospitals, they direct the houses of refuge, in order to lead back to penance those who have wandered from the path of virtue; they receive the charge of the destitute orphans, in order to instruct them in piety and habituate them to labor.

They keep schools for the instruction and education of young female children in those places where there are no other religious to attend to them.

They visit the sick and imprisoned as often as it may be required of them; they exhort them to penance and resignation; they pray for them, and ask alms for them from the faithful; they make soups for them and prepare the medical remedies ordered by the physicians. If their resources permit, they endeavor to keep a supply of the remedies which are ordinarily needed by the sick poor.

They carefully watch over those young

females, who being unprotected or unprovided for, are exposed to lose their virtue; they try to harbor them or provide them with such employment as may procure for them support. Those who have fallen into crime, they labor to bring back to penance; they place them in houses of refuge, or remove them to distant places.

They take a special care of those young females, who, arrived at a certain age, commence to enter society, in order to impress on them the fear of God, to inspire them with Christian modesty and other virtues, so necessary for them in their intercourse with the people of the world. With this view, they induce these young persons to frequent their houses, and teach them those works which are suitable to their state.

They establish Congregations or Sodalities of mercy in those places where none exist; they admit into them ladies of the world, widows, and unmarried females. The assemblies of persons of the world are held at least once a month, for the purpose of visiting and assisting the sick of the parish. Those of the widows and unmarried females are held on Sundays and other festival days, but the widows meet apart from the young unmarried persons. In all these assemblies, the works of mercy must invariably be treated of. Questions of a spiritual nature are also to be introduced, as the duties of persons in their respective states of life; a good rule of life; the means of perseverance; the means of procuring the greater glory of God; the salvation of one's family and neighbor.

In order the better to conduct these sodalities of mercy, the Sisters may consult the Bishop or the Spiritual Father for rules, by which the persons attending them may regulate their conduct. That the Sisters may preserve and increase the zeal necessarily required in performing with fervor and in bearing with courage, all that is difficult and revolting in serving their neighbor, they should persuade themselves of this point, as of an article of Faith, that it is Jesus Christ himself whom they serve, that all those whom they assist are truly the members of the mystical Body of Jesus Christ, and that He who receives all their services, will, on the day of judgment, say to them these most consoling words: "Come, ye Blessed of my Father, possess you the Kingdom prepared for you from the foundation of the world. For I was hungry, and you gave me to eat: I was thirsty, and you gave me to drink: I was a stranger, and you took me in: naked, and you covered me: sick, and you visited me: I was in prison, and you came to me."*

---

* Matt. 25.

What Sister is there, who meditating on these words of Christ, will not feel herself animated to redoubled fervor?

CHAPTER IV.

OF THE CHARITY THE SISTERS OUGHT TO PRACTISE TOWARDS ONE ANOTHER.

The great Apostle St. Paul, says: "Whilst we have time, let us work good to all men, but especially to those who are of the household of the faith." * To put in practice this admonition of the Apostle, it is not sufficient to exercise charity towards the poor stranger; the Sisters of this Congregation should particularly exercise it towards one another; since they are united not only by the same faith, but also by the profession of the same manner of life; are formed into one body in the same Congregation in order that, like the primitive Christians, they may possess but one soul in God. To establish and maintain this perfect union and charity amongst themselves, they shall faithfully follow all the rules which are prescribed in this, and the two succeeding chapters.

They should often recall to mind the following words of Christ, and such others of similar import, which He so frequently repeated to His disciples: " A new command-

---
* Galat. 6.

ment I give unto you: that ye love one another, as I have loved you, that you also love one another."* They should consider this as an inviolable precept, to be observed for the love of Jesus Christ; because He has made it the distinctive mark of His true disciples. They should love one another with as much ardor, zeal, patience and constancy as this Divine Saviour has loved them, notwithstanding their manifold defects.

Nor is it sufficient to possess this charity in the heart; it is, moreover, necessary that it be manifest exteriorly by a general sweetness and amiable condescension of manner, which prompts the truly charitable to be all to all.

They should have an ardent desire for the advancement of one another; a sincere joy at seeing others progress in virtue; a special solicitude for the perfection of others, and afford one another mutual aid by edifying examples, by prayer, and, if Superior, by prudent admonitions.

The truly charitable will yield up their own conveniences to those of a Sister; will aid one another in their necessities; will console one another by demonstrations of true benevolence and friendship; and will never allow their hearts to be infested by sentiments of

---
* John, 13.

jealousy, suspicion, or distrust towards one another.

They should therefore, never utter towards one another words of severity or reproach; of complaint or scorn; they should never manifest by signs, gestures or looks, anything that could indicate the slightest antipathy, or even coldness.

Should it unfortunately happen that a Sister were to violate charity, and offend another in the slightest degree, though not through malice, she should immediately, when made aware of it, humbly and unfeignedly ask pardon of her Sister whom she had offended; and, if both be in fault, the satisfaction should in that case be mutual. Such acts of satisfaction are the best guarantees for the future preservation of charity.

The Sisters should remember that they have the honor of being the spouses of Jesus Christ, the temples of the Holy Ghost; and consequently should show the greatest respect towards one another; and treat one another on all occasions, and in all places, with all modesty, civility and decorum.

Most especially shall they carefully avoid, whatever be the pretext, all particular friendships; neither shall they ever caress, embrace, kiss, or touch one another. However innocently such marks of affection may occur among lay persons, amongst religious they are contrary to the sanctity of their state, and the purity of life of which they make profession. They are, nevertheless, allowed to salute, with a kiss, a new or strange Sister, or one whom they may not have seen for some time.

CHAPTER V.

OF THE CARE OF SICK AND DYING SISTERS.

The Superior of each house shall take care not only to provide, according to the means of the house, everything that is requisite in point of clothing, food, and the comfortable maintenance of all the Sisters; but she should have a more special solicitude for those who are sick. All the Sisters should then redouble their fervor and charity; so that the orders of the physician be most punctually observed; and every kindness and watchfulness afforded them.

As soon as any Sister is seriously sick, the physician shall be called to visit her, and she shall follow his prescriptions and those of the infirmarian. The Confessor shall also be called, and he shall visit the sick Sister from time to time; in order to inspire her, as well with sentiments of penance, patience, submission to the Divine Will, indifference to life, and an ardent desire of being united forever with God. The Superior shall also visit her every day, as often as shall be necessary, in order to console and encourage her to suffer with patience.

Sisters who have habitual infirmities must carefully avoid all caprices and over-anxiety in the adoption of new remedies; and even should not seek for those delicacies which the physician does not order as necessary, and which serve frequently only to promote sensuality and flatter the fancy.

When the sickness augments, and assumes the appearance of approaching death, the Superior shall appoint a Sister to watch both day and night with the infirm person; she shall also procure for her all the usual Sacraments, before she lose her faculties, and shall frequently recommend her soul to the Almighty, on which occasion all the Sisters shall assist. When she shall have expired, all the Sisters assembled around the bed of the deceased, shall pray to the God of all mercy for the repose of her soul.

CHAPTER VI.

OF CHARITY TOWARDS THE DECEASED SISTERS.

As soon as a Sister has expired, the Superior shall give orders to have the corpse dressed out with a black habit, and cap, placed in a coffin, with hands joined together, and a crucifix between them, hanging from the neck, and being thus arranged, it shall be brought to the Chapel or placed in a room.

The Superior shall then assemble all the Sisters at a convenient hour around the coffin, to recite the Office of the Dead, namely Matins and Lauds, or in its stead, may be said the Rosary of the Dead, reciting the 129th Psalm. "From the depths have I cried to thee O Lord," on the large beads; and saying the words: *"Eternal rest grant them, O Lord, and let perpetual light shine upon them,"* on each of the small beads. As far as it may be convenient, let the Sisters, in succession to one another, watch with the corpse, and pray for the deceased until the interment take place.

When the time of interment is come, four Sisters shall bear the coffin to the cemetery, provided it be attached to their house; and the others shall accompany it, walking two and two; holding lighted tapers in their hands. The Superior shall take care that all be conducted with decorum and solemnity. She shall, also, procure a Solemn Mass, or, at least, a low one on the day of decease, also on the thirtieth day, and the anniversary day. On these days, the Sisters shall offer up a communion, and say the Office or Rosary of the Dead for their deceased Sister.

The deceased of the Congregation shall always be interred in the burial place of the house, if there be one attached to it; or, if not, in that of the Parish.

On the decease of any Sister, the Superior

shall give immediate notice of it to all the Superiors of houses, in the various dioceses; and the Superior of each house shall have the Office or Rosary of the Dead said in the community for the deceased. All the Sisters shall offer up a communion for her, and sha l also recommend her soul to God in their private devotions.

The Superior shall get a Mass celebrated in each month for the repose of all those Sisters who may have died during that year.

On the decease of a Sister, the Superior shall register, in the book of the house, the day, the hour, and year of her death ; also, her name, age, and time of her profession in the Congregation, together with her other qualities.

PART III.

Of the form for receiving Sisters, and of the qualifications required in order to be received into the Congregation.

CHAPTER I.

OF THE RECEPTION OF NOVICES.

The choice of persons to be received into the Congregation is a matter of the greatest importance; as a community cannot be maintained in the state of perfection which it professes, unless the persons who compose it possess the dispositions required for the attainment of its object. Hence, the Superior, and even the Sisters, shall proceed to the reception of postulants with the greatest prudence; and shall, accordingly, observe the following rules:

When a candidate for admission into the Congregation presents herself, the Superior, accompanied by another Sister, shall examine her in private as to her country, her parents, her age, habits, health, occupations during life; her trade, if she have any; and as to the motives which induce her to apply for admission into the Congregation. She shall also carefully observe her appearance, and make inquiries respecting her; and should she be found not to have the qualities required in a Sister, she shall politely reject her application. If she appear to possess the necessary qualifications, the Superior shall, by giving her some encouragement, refer her to another time, in order, hereby, to try her perseverance.

But, after she has been sufficiently tried, and when the Superior, having taken the advice of the Sisters, shall judge her to be a fit person to be received, she shall ask the permission of the Bishop, or of the Spiritual Father, to receive her into the house for trial. She shall then admit her into the house, where she shall remain at least three months, if it should appear necessary, for her trial; and, during this time, she shall retain her secular dress, perform all the duties of the Sisters; except that she shall not assist in Chapter; and she shall go to communion only on Sundays and the principal festivals. During this time, the Superior and the Sisters shall diligently observe her conduct, shall try her, and give her, with all charity, those admonitions for her correction and spiritual improvement, which may be deemed necessary.

The time of trial being terminated, the Superior shall assemble all the Sisters in Chapter, at which the Aspirant shall assist on bended knees. The Superior shall read, or cause to be read, the chapter on the reception of Novices, and the following one containing the qualities of Novices. After which she shall declare to her that: 1st. She is obliged to acknowledge whether she judge herself possessed of the qualities expressed in these chapters; and, 2ndly, that, if during her novitiate, or even after her profession, it be discovered that she has any of the defects mentioned in the same chapter, it will be necessary to dismiss her from the Congregation, as one who had entered it through fraud.

When she has replied to all the points, and to such other questions respecting her intentions and resolutions, she shall retire from the Chapter room, and the Superior shall take the votes of the Sisters for the admission of the candidate. If she obtain more than half the votes, she shall be admitted to receive the habit; and shall afterwards be examined by the Bishop, or by the Spiritual Father, or such other person as they shall appoint. If, after the examination, she be judged suitable for the Congregation, she shall receive the habit, with the accustomed ceremonies, and the Superior shall then register the act of her réception, in the book destined for that purpose, and cause the signatures of the Sisters to be affixed.

CHAPTER II.

OF THE QUALITIES REQUIRED IN THOSE ADMITTED TO THE NOVITIATE.

As the Sisters of the Congregation cannot observe enclosure, and must have intercourse with the world in the discharge of the exercises of charity and the works of mercy, it is highly necessary that none be received into it but such as have the necessary qualities, not only to acquit themselves of their arduous employments, but also to preserve the most perfect decorum and a firmness of virtue which may always edify persons of the world. The following are the qualities and virtues which they should possess in order to be received:

1. They should be born in lawful wedlock, and be baptized. They should accordingly bring with them the certificate of their baptism. It is required that their parents should have enjoyed a favorable reputation; and should they be under repute of any grievous crime, or have been condemned in any criminal cause, they shall not be received.

2. Their life must have been edifying and virtuous; for should they have been scandalous in their life, they shall on no account be admitted.

3. They should enjoy good health, and have the strength necessary for the discharge of the duties of the Congregation, which are

rather severe. Those therefore who have any chronic or contagious disease, or who are of weakly constitution, or who are blind, maimed, or very much disfigured, are not to be admitted.

4. They should possess good judgment, and be capable of filling the temporal and spiritual offices entrusted to them.

5. Those whose dispositions are not mild and inclined to virtue, should not be admitted; as also the passionate, proud, inconstant, idle, and those who are indifferent about the things of God. If there be a prospect that certain dispositions may be corrected, as in time of probation many great changes and improvements have occurred, those therefore who are seriously intent on their amendment may be received.

6. They should be perfectly free from all pecuniary or other obligations; neither should they be under any obligation of assisting or supporting their parents. Hence, those who have not previously discharged their debts, and whose parents cannot subsist without their aid, cannot be received.

7. None shoud be received before the age of fifteen completed, or over thirty-five years; because persons should understand well the nature and obligations of the state they embrace. They should also possess sufficient strength to fulfil its duties and a mind submissive to all the obligations of obe-

dience, which is not easily to be met with in those who are advanced in age.

8. Young widows may be received, provided they have no charge of children, who are not already settled, and if they have no excessive attachment for them. Such persons not unfrequently appear very ardent for a time, but afterwards experience great disquietude of mind for having left their family. Hence they require to be put off for a longer time than others in order to examine their vocation. When received, they should go out but rarely, lest they revive within themselves the spirit of the world which they have renounced.

CHAPTER III.

OF THE NOVITIATE AND EDUCATION OF THE NOVICES.

The Novices shall remain two years in the novitiate before their profession. Though the time cannot be shortened, it may be prolonged by the Bishop or Spiritual Father; but always for very weighty motives.

Novices can be professed in any house of the Congregation; but if convenient, it would be desirable that each Bishop were to establish in his diocese a suitable, spacious house, where the community would be more numerous, in order to perform the exercises of the Congregation with more effect, and therein to train up the Novices more regularly.

Before taking the habit, the Sisters ought to make a general confession of their whole life, that being established in perfect peace of mind, they may begin a new life in the service of God. If they have already made one, they should at least make a review since the last general confession.

The Novices ought to be inflamed with fervor of the Holy Ghost, like all who have abandoned the world for the service of God. In order to preserve and increase this holy fervor, they should resolve scrupulously to observe all these Constitutions, without the least relaxation; for the Holy Spirit assures us, that "He who despises small things, shall fall by little and little."* They should love and esteem their state and their vocation, because the Almighty has called them to it, and have unbounded confidence and entire submission to their Superiors and Mistresses, and entertain respect and friendship for all their Sisters.

Care shall be taken that they serve in all the employments, and practice all the exercises of the Congregation, as in the kitchen, the attendance on the sick, care of the schools, and so of the rest. They may also accompany a Sister in visiting the sick and

---

* Eccl. 19.

the poor; and, excepting on such occasions, they shall never go out, except in cases of great necessity, and always accompanied by a Sister. Neither shall they receive the visits of lay persons, except with the permission of the Superior or Mistress of Novices, who, as far as possible, shall be present on such occasions, or send some one in her place.

They shall assist on all Fridays at the Chapter of the Superior; and having heard what is to be told to them, they shall tell their faults. They leave the Chapter before the Sisters tell theirs.

When the Novices have remained a year in the novitiate, the Superior shall assemble the Chapter, and shall ask each sister her opinion respecting the Novices; and, having heard all, and received the relation of the Mistress of Novices, if any Novice be judged unsuitable for the Congregation, she shall be sent home; but if she be approved of by at least the half of those present, she shall be allowed to complete her novitiate.

A month before the end of the novitiate, the Superior shall assemble the Chapter, in which the same ceremonies shall be observed as at the reception of Novices. She shall call them, and represent to them the obligations they are under of answering faithfully to all the questions to be put to them. She shall then examine them on all the qualities **and** defects as given in Chapter II., which shall be read to them; and she shall remind them that if, after their profession, they should be found to have given deceitful answers, they will be put out of the Congregation as having entered it fraudulently.

Having received their answers, the Superior shall cause them to leave the Chapter, and shall receive the votes of the Sisters. Those Novices who shall have received the majority of votes shall be admitted to their profession; those who shall not have received more than half the number of votes, shall be sent home, and their worldly clothes and other effects which they brought to the house with them, shall be given to them, deducting for their board, during their probation and novitiate.

When the Novices shall be approved of by the Chapter, as worthy to be admitted to their profession, the Superior shall acquaint the Bishop or the Spiritual Father, in order that he may examine them, and receive their profession, in case he deem them fit subjects; or appoint some priest to receive their profession, according as he may determine.

CHAPTER IV.

OF THE PROFESSION AND OF THE VOWS OF THE SISTERS.

There is no sacrifice which man can make

to God, so holy, so precious, and so agreeable to the Divine Majesty, as that included in the three vows of perpetual poverty, chastity, and obedience, by which he gives up all that he has, and all that he is. To prepare themselves for this great sacrifice, Novices should make a retreat of eight or ten days, before their profession. During these days, they should occupy their minds exclusively in meditating on the excellence and sacredness of the vows they are about to take, as also the obligations to which these vows bind them in the Congregation. They should also examine their consciences with great exactness, in order that, before making an offering of themselves to God, they may purify themselves by such a confession as their Confessor may advise.

At the end of the retreat, the Novices shall, in the presence of the Bishop, or spiritual Father, or other priest appointed for that purpose, make their profession by the simple vows of poverty, chastity and obedience in the Congregation of Saint Joseph; and, at the same time, promise to God, on all occasions, to practise the most profound humility, and the most perfect charity towards their neighbor.

After taking these vows, they shall themselves write the act of their profession in a book exclusively kept for that purpose. They shall subscribe it, and obtain the signature of the Bishop or other ecclesiastic before whom the profession was made; and also of two or three witnesses, who were present. Should the professed not know how to write, the act of profession shall be written by another; and they shall make the sign of the cross with the pen at the bottom of the act, in the place of their signature. The form of the profession, and of the act to be inscribed in the book, is given at the end of the Directory.

The professed Sisters should especially bear in mind the duties to which they have bound themselves, and the obligation they have contracted of constantly aspiring to perfection. As this perfection consists in the perfect observance of their vows, and of the Constitutions, they should devote all their energies to this object.

CHAPTER V.

OF THE VOWS OF OBEDIENCE.

The Spirit of God assures us, in the Holy Scriptures, that the sacrifice of obedience exceeds all other sacrifices. Samuel said: "Doth the Lord desire holocausts and victims, and not rather that the voice of the Lord should be obeyed? for obedience is better than sacrifices."* The reason is,

---

* 1. King, 15.

by obedience we sacrifice our understanding and our will, which is a more precious offering in the sight of God than anything else we can part with. Hence we should infer, that as there is no greater virtue in religion than perpetual obedience to the will of God, so there is no greater sin than disobedience to the Divine Will.

The Sisters, therefore, should have an extraordinary esteem for this virtue, which they have vowed to the Almighty, and they should prefer it to all other virtues. Hence they should take care to observe it with extreme exactness, even on the most trivial occasions. They should have a mortal hatred of disobedience, and avoid with solicitude the slightest appearance thereof.

There are two kinds of obedience in the Congregation, the one general, the other particular. The general consists in doing all that is prescribed in the Constitutions; the particular consists in doing whatever is commanded by the Superiors. To comply with their vow of obedience, the Sisters should perform promptly, exactly, willingly, and joyfully, whatever the Constitutions prescribe, and the Superiors order for their perfection, and for the temporal and spiritual welfare of the Congregation.

No superior can order anything to be done which is contrary to the Constitutions. Should any difficulty arise concerning any of them, or concerning any statute contained in them, the Bishop shall be consulted, and his decision shall be conclusive.

If any Sister should feel great difficulty in doing what is ordered, either on account of infirmity or any other reason, she may, respectfully, and with all due humility, propose such reasons to the Superior. This being done she should submit her judgment and will to whatever shall be ordered, and obey with utmost willingness. Should she still experience any repugnance, she should, in imitation of Jesus Christ, endeavor to overcome it. In His mysterious agony, He contended with such violence and courage against the repugnance which His human will felt at the sight of the torments of His Passion, that the Evangelist tells us: "His soul was sorrowful even unto death;"* and again: "His sweat became as drops of blood, trickling down upon the ground." † But he overcame all these repugnances and submitted entirely to the Will of His Divine Father, saying: "Father! not as I will, but as Thou wilt." ‡ After which he went forward willingly and courageously to meet those who came to apprehend Him.

The Sisters should also remember that, in observing the Constitutions and obeying their Superiors, they are most certainly doing the

---

* Matt. 26. † Luke, 22. ‡ Matt. and Luke.

will of God; while on the other hand, they are not doing the Divine Will, but opposing it, if they act against obedience, or choose for themselves what they will do.

Should a Sister refuse to obey, and persist in her disobedience, the Superior shall remonstrate with her, in the most charitable manner, and shall give her some time to reflect on her conduct. She can also send another Sister, whom she may judge a proper person, to bring her to a sense of her duty, and the Community should also offer up their fervent prayers for one who is in such imminent danger of losing her vocation and her soul. If all means, which patience and charity can suggest, prove ineffectual, and she continue obstinate, the Superior shall acquaint the Bishop or the Spiritual Father of the circumstance, in order that suitable penance be imposed on her, or, if deemed advisable, that she be dismissed from the Community.

CHAPTER VI.

OF THE VOW OF CHASTITY.

Virgins are compared to the angels of God; hence the Sisters of St. Joseph, who have made a vow of chastity, should in a manner live in the Congregation, as the angels live in Heaven; that is, like true and faithful spouses of Christ, their life should be quite interior, spiritual, and devoted to the love of God, and remote from everything earthly. They should, therefore, preserve themselves, as much as possible, in the constant presence of God. They should observe, in all things, and on all occasions, great modesty, and the strictest restraint over all their senses; they should shun every action, word, thought, or look, contrary in the slightest degree to holy modesty; as also, all useless conversations with persons of the other sex. They should also carefully avoid all those familiarities and caresses amongst one another, which natural and sensual friendship might suggest.

They should often call to mind that they have the honor of being the daughters of St. Joseph, and in order to be worthy of this quality, they should imitate the incomparable purity of this holy Patriarch, and of Mary ever Virgin, his most holy spouse. Finally, their whole mind, their heart, their thoughts words, actions, looks, and entire deportment, should breathe an air of celestial purity and chastity. And as, according to the Holy Spirit: "No one can be continent unless the Lord give it,"* so they should ask this invaluable favor of Him, from whose bounty it must come, most especially in all tempta-

---

* Wisd. 8.

tions and dangers to which they may be exposed.

The Sisters should have the most filial confidence in the protection of the most Blessed Virgin and of St. Joseph, who most assuredly will obtain of God for them perseverance in this virtue.

If Superiors see that any Sister permit herself, in the slightest degree, to use words, sing profane songs, or indulge in dangerous readings, familiarity or caresses between one another, looks or deportment in any way unbecoming a virgin consecrated to God, they shall promptly admonish such Sister thereof; and if she do not immediately correct the fault, suitable penance should be imposed.

If, unhappily, which may God avert, any Sister were fully convicted of having voluntarily violated her vow of chastity, she shall be unhesitatingly dismissed from the Congregation.

CHAPTER VII.

OF THE VOW OF POVERTY.

The poverty which Jesus Christ counsels in the Gospel to those who desire to be perfect, requires that they should leave, both in effect and in inclination, all the goods of the world; hence, to keep their vow of poverty, the Sisters should effectually give up all their goods, by leaving them to their relatives or to the poor, or by resigning them to the Superiors of the Congregation. They should renounce all secret inclinations towards them, so that they may feel a most complete contempt of all worldly possessions, or at least be indifferent to them. They should not have even an attachment to the temporal or spiritual things they make use of in supplying their temporal wants, or in the exercises of piety; such as their habit, linen, room, books, pictures, beads, or such other things.

The vow of poverty disqualifies them from having a right to anything, and, consequently, they cannot, under any pretext whatever, give away or receive anything, without the permission of the Superior; and should they have accepted of anything, they must place it at the disposal of the Superior, to be employed as she may judge fit. To banish all idea of property, the Sisters of St. Joseph should not make use of the word *mine*, when speaking of the things which they use. Thus, instead of saying: *my* dress, *my* room, *my* book; they shall always say: *our* dress, *our* room, *our* book, and so of the rest.

For the more perfect observance of this vow, and that the Sisters may have no pretext for receiving or procuring anything for their own use, because it may appear absolutely necessary, we order all Superiors to procure and furnish for all the Sisters of their

Communities, as far as the means of the house will permit, whatever is required in point of diet and dress, in health and sickness, without any distinction or preference. If the Superior should neglect or refuse to give the Sisters what is necessary for them, according to the means of the establishment, she shall be severely corrected or even punished by the Bishop or Spiritual Father, according to her fault; and should she continue the same, she shall be deprived of her charge.

That the Sisters may appropriate nothing to themselves of those things which are necessary for their support, it is enjoined that the habits, linen, food and generally all things that are required for support and clothing, be placed in common under the care of a Sister, appointed by the Superior, who shall distribute them equally and without any distinction, according as they are wanted.

If what is given to the Sisters be not as good as they would desire; or if anything necessary should be wanting, they ought to remember that Jesus Christ their Master, passed his whole life in poverty; as also, that their vow of poverty binds them to lead a poor life, in which all superfluity should be avoided; that they should be content with what is merely necessary; and, finally, they should suffer with p'easure, or, at least, with patience, and in the genuine spirit of poverty, when anything is wanting, even of the things that might appear necessary.

The Superior shall take special care that the rooms, the furniture, tables, dresses, and linen of the Sisters shall be of a simple, modest, and poor character. They shall retrench whatever in these matters seems superfluous and contrary to simplicity. No silver shall be allowed for use, unless it be for the Church, with the exception of silver spoons, which are allowed, in imitation of St. Francis of Sales, who allowed them to the Nuns of the Visitation.

If any Sister commit a fault against her vow of poverty, by receiving, keeping or giving away anything, without the permission of the Superior, she shall be punished as guilty of theft, and in proportion to the grievousness of the fault.

It is a custom permitted in our Congregation as well as in others, that Sisters, by their last will and testament, can dispose of whatever they have brought with them to the Congregation, or which may have been given to them while in it.

Sisters cannot make their last will without the permission of the Spiritual Father, or of the Superior of the house in which they reside; and in no case shall they make their will except in favor of some Sister belonging to the house where they dwell, unless the Spiritual Father or the Superior deem it advisable that it be made in favor of some Sister of another house of the Congregation.

In giving permission to Sisters to make a will, and to receive inheritances, it is not at all intended to exempt them from the observance of their vow of poverty; for all those who shall receive any inheritance are bound to resign it immediately into the hands of the Superior, who shall dispose of it just as of any other property belonging to the house for the advantage of the Community. It is, therefore, prohibited to any Sister, who may receive an inheritance, property or goods, to dispose of it, or them, either in whole or part, for themselves, or for their parents, or friends, or other persons whomsoever, without the express permission of the Superior. The infraction of this vow shall be considered an injustice.

PART IV.

Special Regulations for the Officers and for their Election, and General Rules for all the Sisters.

However holy the rules of these Constitutions may be, and the maxims of virtue professed in our Congregation of St. Joseph, if the Superior and other Officers are not diligent in having them observed; and if they have no rules by which they themselves should be guided, for the due discharge of their respective duties, it cannot long maintain itself. For this purpose, we shall, in this Fourth Part, lay down the special rules of the Superior and of the Officers, together with the general rules of all the Sisters; which will contain all the duties of both Superiors and Sisters, and will enable all to walk in the way of Christian perfection, and mutually to assist one another in attaining that sanctity which God demands of them.

CHAPTER I.

RULES FOR THE SUPERIOR.

1. The Superior ought to be persuaded that she holds the place of God, and is ap-

pointed by His Supreme Will and Goodness, to co-operate with Him in governing the Congregation of St. Joseph; and as she will certainly receive from Him praise and reward for her success, so she shall be responsible for any loss or ruin that may be the consequence of her misconduct or neglect. She should, therefore, undertake this charge with great fear and humility.

2. She cannot, of her own strength, maintain in fervor a Community which professes to aspire to such high degree of perfection, and which undertakes every exercise of charity and work of mercy. She must, then, often have recourse to the Almighty by prayer, and she should labor, by the most profound humility, by the most exact correspondence with the graces of the Holy Ghost, and by the most intimate union with God, to become worthy of His graces.

3. In order to lead her daughters to the perfection she desires of them, and to render them exact in the observance of the rules of the Institute, she should, as far as she is able, with the Divine aid, excel in the example of a holy life, and in the most perfect obedience to all the orders of the Institute.

4. She should frequently pray, and even with sighs and tears, for those under her care; and carefully considering the conduct of all, thank the Divine Goodness for the progress made by fervent subjects, and to

endeavor to augment it; and by tears to expiate the defects and sins of the imperfect, and to apply the suitable remedies.

5. Besides general watchfulness over all the Sisters, she should be perfectly acquainted with the conduct of the several under-officers of the house, and see if union and charity reign, and if the rules be strictly observed.

6. As prayer and union with God maintain and strengthen souls in all virtues, she shall pay strict attention, and examine whether all the Sisters exercise themselves in these virtues; whether they observe a great spirit of recollection, which alone can maintain this union, and which greatly edifies all persons who see them and treat with them.

7. She should show forth, on all occasions, a spirit of humility, mildness, and charity, that it may evidently appear she does not allow herself to be guided by humor or passion, but by the spirit of these three virtues: which, however, should not prevent her from firmly and courageously insisting on the exact observance of all the rules of the Institute. The Superior should make no exception of persons, but perseveringly procure the execution of what she has once ordered, for the greater glory of God, unless evident reasons oblige her to change the first orders given.

8. She should overlook no fault which comes to her knowledge, but try to correct it, either by a public penance, if public edification require it, or by some admonition, but always with marks of sincere maternal affection. She should always manifest extraordinary solicitude for all the Sisters in their wants and necessities, by charitably and affectionately supplying them with whatever they may require.

9. She should avoid all austere and imperious manners in giving commands, and rather appear to supplicate her daughters as fellow-sisters; which is also more in accordance with the mildness and humility of the Gospel of Jesus Christ.

10. She should remember that her character of Superior, instead of raising her above others, rather humbles her; as it makes her the servant of the servants of Jesus Christ. Hence she should respect all those who are under her, and, as far as possible, she should study their good pleasure as much as her own.

11. Besides the constant solicitude for the good order of the house, she shall assemble her council once a week, and confer with those who compose it, concerning all that passes in the Community; and all that regards charity towards the poor, who should be specially dear to her.

12. She shall ordinarily call to these con-

sultations the Assistant, the two Counsellors, and the Procuratrix; and when she thinks fit, she can call others. She shall simply propose the matters for consultation, with the reasons on both sides, without showing any inclination more for one than the other side of the question, that the Sisters may be more entirely at liberty to give their opinions on the matter proposed.

13. In consultations of any moment, before determining anything, after having heard the matter proposed, all shall kneel down and recite the hymn of the Holy Ghost, and employ about a half-quarter of an hour in prayer, to beg of God to enable them to resolve the case according to His most holy Will.

14. Extreme care should be used in the choice of candidates for admission into the Congregation; and none are to be admitted except such as possess the qualities mentioned in the Third Part of this Institute. The Superior should firmly oppose those who would appear inclined to admit all sorts of persons into the Congregation. Should any have been admitted, having any of the more important defects mentioned in the Third Part, she should dismiss them as soon as possible; particularly, if the habits contracted be such as to leave little hope of their being eradicated without great difficulty.

15. She shall watch with special care over the Novices, in order that they may be trained up with the true spirit of the Congregation; sincerely intent on their greater perfection in all things, and most diligent in the observance of the Constitutions.

16. In order to acquit herself still more perfectly of the duties of her office, the Superior can ask her Counsellors, from time to time, to point out to her the faults she may have committed, and also to mention if the Community have any complaints against her; and thus by correcting herself to become a model for all.

17. She shall take special care of all papers, such as title-deeds, contracts, and other documents of importance to the establishment, and shall register in due order all such papers in a book to be kept for that purpose; so that in case of necessity they may be promptly found. All these papers shall be kept in a chest with three keys, one of which shall be consigned to the three following persons: one to the Superior, another to the Assistant, and the third to the Procuratrix. In the same chest shall be deposited whatever money may happen to be in the house, and which is not wanted for the current expenses of the establishment.

18. She shall not allow any Sister, through vanity or levity, to change the color or form of the dress, or permit them to let their hair

grow for an ornament, or suffer them to wear false hair. On the contrary, they should always observe the simplicity and humility of dress as prescribed in the First Part of these Constitutions.

19. She shall hold a Chapter on Friday of each week, for the correction and amendment of faults, and all the Sisters shall assist thereat, and declare their faults.

20. She shall hold, every Sunday, a conference of all the Sisters, in which they shall speak of those things which regard the welfare of the house of the Congregation, or of their souls.

21. She shall keep a seal, of oval form, and about the ordinary size of seals, bearing engraved the bust of St. Joseph, having the Infant Jesus in his arms, and with this inscription: *"Superior of the house of Sisters of Saint Joseph."* It shall be used for sealing her letters and those of the Sisters.

CHAPTER II.

RULES FOR THE ASSISTANT.

She supplies the place of the Superior, in certain circumstances; she ought to aid her in the exercise of her office and in the management of the whole Community.

1. She shall have a special care of the exterior management of the Community, by

seeing that all the persons of the house be provided with everything they require; giving, in this respect, proofs of the most cordial charity and attentive watchfulness. Secondly, by seeing carefully to all the offices, to the rooms and other places of the house, that poverty, decorum, and cleanliness be everywhere observed. Thirdly, by watching over the cooking and other things necessary for the support of life; giving orders, with all charity, to those in the different offices, that they provide for these things at the appointed hours, and in a suitable manner. Fourthly, respecting the order of the daily actions, that they be performed at the appointed hours, in the places, and according to the regulations of the Constitutions. Fifthly, to see to the observance of all the rules, particularly those that regard the exterior disposition of things, as silence, decorum, and such like things.

2. To acquit herself more faithfully of her office, she ought, in the morning, to review these points just laid down, in order to see if there be anything to provide for, or to correct; and in the evening, she ought to foresee what may be necessary to have done on the following day, for the well ordering of the house, and even if necessary, to note down in writing what may be of particular moment, that it be not omitted.

3. She shall have a book, where she shall

mark down in order, the furniture of the house generally, and of the respective apartments separately; and once a year she shall verify and examine them, in company with the Superior, to see what may have suffered injury, in order to have it repaired, or what may have perished, to have it replaced.

4. At the commencement of each month, and of the different seasons, she shall examine the said articles, and shall visit the rooms of the Sisters, to inquire about the state of their health, and charitably to provide for all their necessities.

5. She shall frequently visit the apartments and offices of the house, and see that order be kept in them, and that the Community be duly supplied with the necessary provisions.

6. She shall take special care of the sick, seeing that they want nothing, and they be charitably attended, both as regards the soul and body, without any sparing of expenses.

7. She shall charitably provide for the necessities of the Superior; and in case of her having neglected herself, she shall have power to order her, having previously consulted on the matter with the Counsellors, to adopt the remedies deemed necessary, both for her health and comfort.

Finally, she shall, with the Divine aid, in all things, as far as may be possible, maintain such a spirit of order and piety, as is conformable to the lives of persons aspiring to and making profession of the most **sublime** virtue.

CHAPTER III.

RULES WHICH REGARD THE CO-ADJUTRIX; WHO SHALL BE MISTRESS OF NOVICES.

1. As the duty of the Assistant is to assist the Superior in the exterior management of the house, so that of the Co-adjutrix is to assist in all that regards the spiritual conduct of the Novices, in order to lead them to the perfection of their state.

2. The end of her office shall be, to instruct and train up all the Sisters under her charge, in the knowledge of spiritual matters, and to see that they practise, with the greatest exactness, even the minutest regulations and observances of their Constitutions.

3. To attain this end, which is so important, she shall have a special care of the education of the candidates for admission, of the Novices, and of the newly professed, for two years after their profession. She shall endeavor to excite in them an efficacious desire of their perfection.

4. In this undertaking she shall conduct them gradually to the perfection of the Institute, as persons do not at once become perfect, and practise the most elevated maxims of virtue.

5. She shall carefully examine each one's disposition, in order to correct what may be defective, and to encourage and improve what may be good and serviceable for the glory of God. She should specially study what in each one is the movement of Divine grace, and the road by which the Holy Spirit draws each Sister, that so she may cultivate those movements of grace, and not train persons necessarily according to her own notions and practices of virtue and perfection.

6. She should be mild and kind towards all the Sisters, that she may thus gain their confidence, and be enabled to train them to perfection.

7. In the commencement of the novitiate, she shall endeavor by conferences, and by proposing the examples of our predecessors, and other motives of virtue, to excite in them an ardent desire of great sanctity, and to impress on their minds that the daughters of St. Joseph aspire in all things to the highest perfection; equally as if they made an express vow to that effect.

8. To conduct them to so sublime an end, she should let them understand, that it must be effected by the Divine Grace, and that as it is not granted, except to the meek and humble, they should above all things become profoundly humble.

9. She should lead them to a perfect denial

of themselves, and of all their vicious inclinations, in order that the grace of God may reign in them; and to facilitate this great work, she shall show them that there is nothing nobler than to overcome oneself for God; and that He communicates His consolations to those who courageously take up their cross to follow Jesus.

10. She shall lead them to the most perfect correspondence with the grace of God, instructing them to accuse themselves of the smallest fault in this particular.

11. She shall study with special care to comprehend well and to practise the maxims of virtue, as given at the end of these Constitutions; and she should also try to insinuate the love and practice of the same to the Sisters for the greater glory of God.

12. She should hold conferences with the professed Sisters every fortnight, and with the Novices once a week, whom she shall teach how to make known with sincerity the state of their interior, and to confide in their Director, their Superior, and in the Mistress of Novices.

13. Above all things, she should instruct them in the exercise of meditation, and facilitate and sweeten its practise to them, as nothing is more important in the Institute, and more essential for their own perfection.

14. She shall, with special care, expound

and inculcate to them all that is contained in the Constitutions and Directory regarding the Sacraments, and the ordinary and extraordinary actions of life; together with the manner of assisting one's neighbor in all the exercises of charity becoming their profession.

15. With respect to the newly professed Sisters, she shall try to maintain them in their first fervor, and lead them on sweetly and steadily in the practise of the most perfect virtue.

16. If a Sister be tempted and sad, she should assist her with great sweetness and patience; listening to her with great calmness and affection; and trying with the Divine aid to soothe her, as far as may be possible, and suggest to her the necessary remedies for her temptations. If these efforts do not succeed, she shall, if able, apply to some enlightened and zealous Spiritual Father; but particularly, she shall recommend her to God, and obtain the prayers of others for her.

CHAPTER IV.

REGULATIONS FOR THE PROCURATRIX.

1. The duty of the Procuratrix shall be, to assist the Superior in the temporal management of the house; she should then diligently apply to this duty, so that the Supe-

rior may be more at liberty to devote herself to spiritual affairs.

2. In conducting the affairs of the establishment, and especially in transacting business with strangers, she should remember to seek only the will of God, to recommend all things to Him, discharging all her duties with wonderful calmness and patience; showing in her manner a total detachment from everything worldly; that the reproach, which is but too often made against persons consecrated to God, may not be applied to her — that they often manifest more attachment to worldly things than those who, by their profession, are engaged in them.

3. She should receive, in presence of the Superior, the revenues or other payments, by which the house is maintained; enter the same in a book; as also the disbursements of the house at the close of each month, in order that the state of the house may always be seen.

4. She shall keep a chest, with lock or other means, for keeping the money necessary for the contingent expenses of the house; and should she have a very considerable sum, she should keep it in the chest with the three keys, which ought to be placed in the Superior's room.

5. She should have a book, or a list of the provisions requisite for the Sisters, and the

probable expenses of them; and an entry of the time they are to be bought, by which she shall be guided to make the necessary provision, and at the ordinary prices.

6. If inexperienced in these duties, she shall take advice of others, consulting them with humility, and following their counsels.

7. Having made due provision for the maintenance of the Community, she shall, at least once a month, or more frequently if required, inspect the provisions she may have purchased, in order to see that they suffer no injury.

8. Should the establishment have any differences with any one, respecting temporal matters, the Procuratrix shall with the utmost care avoid all legal proceedings, except in the case of absolute necessity, and refer the matter to the Bishop, or Spiritual Father, or to the Superior. Every other means of amicable arrangement should be had recourse to. If all these efforts prove ineffectual, the matter should be confided to persons of intelligence and probity; and the house should always prefer to suffer some loss, and settle the affair by arbitration, or such like way, rather than to engage in a law-suit.

9. She shall give to the Superior, in presence of her council, every two months, an account of the receipts and expenditures of the house; and at the end of each year she shall

produce a detailed account of the state of the establishment, for the Bishop, or for the Spiritual Father, according as he shall direct.

10. If not able to attend all the minor details of her office, she can employ some person appointed for this purpose by the Superior; such minor expenses shall be entered and as soon as possible, in the Account Book, lest anything should be forgotten.

11. She should see that the Sisters diligently perform the work assigned to them, and make sale of the produce of the work, either for the relief of the poor, or for the support of the house.

12. She should carefully avoid giving any just ground for complaint, in all the matters she shall purchase for the Community; and, however poor the house may be, she should place the most unbounded confidence in God, that He will not allow her to want for anything, when she seeks, in the spirit of true charity, to satisfy her Sisters who have abandoned all things for the love of Jesus Christ.

13. She shall keep an inventory of all the articles which the Novices may bring with them to the house; she shall get them marked by themselves, if they know how to do so; otherwise, the Superior shall mark them. She shall carefully keep and preserve them, **until they make their profession.**

CHAPTER V.

REGULATIONS FOR THE MONITOR.

1. The monitor is appointed to admonish the Superior of her faults, and to receive such complaints as may be made against her.

2. She shall never reprove the Superior, without having consulted God respecting the matter; if it be advisable to do so, as also respecting the manner, time and place of making the correcting with greatest utility. The Superior shall also ask her, from time to time, if she have no complaint to make against her; in order to afford her an opportunity of doing so more easily.

3. She should not be urgent and frequent in making these reproofs, and never without necessity; but always with mildness, humility, and respect; remembering that she is the inferior, and the Superior holds the place of Jesus Christ.

4. The fault observed in the Superior may at times be written down, that she may reflect on it at her leisure, and correct it.

5. When an inferior makes a complaint against the Superior, she shall mildly listen to what is said, without, at the same time, giving entire credit to it; and she shall deliberately enquire about the matter with great prudence, before she admonishes the Superior. The Monitor should carefully soothe those who make complaints; especially if

such complaints appear unreasonable; showing them that they find fault without reason; and when there appears to be some ground for the complaint, she shall hold out the hope that all shall be duly remedied. In case of her inability to remedy the matter, she shall inform the Spiritual Father of it.

CHAPTER VI.

RULES FOR THE COUNSELLORS.

1. The two Counsellors are appointed to aid, by their advice, the Superior in the management of the house, and in whatever concerns the good of the Institute. Hence, they should frequently read and meditate on the Constitutions.

2. If they observe anything contrary to the good order of the Congregation, they should give notice of it to the Superior, in order that it be remedied.

3. They should not make their complaints precipitately, or through passion; but after mature consideration, and from pure zeal for God's glory.

4. When any good thought presents itself to their mind, either for the welfare of the house in which they reside, or of the Congregation at large, they should mark it down, and communicate it to the Superior, in due time and in the proper place.

5. They shall be extremely careful about

the persons admitted into the Congregation of Saint Joseph; and they shall on no account give their vote for any one who does not possess the qualities required by the Constitutions. Should any one be received into it, not having these qualifications, they shall procure her dismissal therefrom, as soon as may be convenient.

6. When called to consult together on any affair, they shall recommend the matter to God by prayer, and shall endeavor to have God alone in view, in all their deliberations and resolutions. They shall try to lay aside all interests and feelings which might blind the judgment, or deprive them of the liberty of deciding according to reason and religion. In all cases of difficulty, they shall vote for that side that presents the least disadvantages, and that promises most for the advancement of the glory of God.

7. If any matter of importance be submitted to their consideration, and they be not able at once to give their opinion, they shall ask for more time to recommend the matter to God, and think on it at their leisure.

8. After the consultation, they shall submit to the judgment of the Superior, letting her take whatever resolution she shall deem most advisable, without either murmuring, or revealing to the other Sisters what transpired in their deliberations.

9. Should they, however, see that the Superior has taken any determination evidently dangerous or pernicious to the Congregation, they shall, in the most discreet manner, inform the Bishop or the Spiritual Father thereof, in order that a remedy be applied.

CHAPTER VII.

RULES FOR THE ATTENDANT ON THE POOR.

1. She shall undertake her office with great zeal, and great desire of discharging it in the best possible way for the relief of the poor.

2. She shall read and apply to her charge a part of the rules for the Procuratrix.

3. She shall keep a small box, secured by a lock, in which to put the money for the poor, which should not be mixed up with that of the community.

4. She shall have a room with lock and key, in which to keep provisions and furniture for the poor, and, if possible, a medicine-chest, to be able to distribute among them the more necessary remedies.

5. She shall keep four books: in one, she shall register the receipts and expenditures of each month; in another, she shall record the temporal and spiritual wants which she and other Sisters may have remarked in the course of their visits; in the third shall be a list of the provisions and furniture in-

tended for the poor; and in the fourth, she shall keep an account of the debts and of the loans made of any furniture, in order to recover the same, or any sum of money that may be a just equivalent therefor.

6. She shall examine the cases of want noted down, in order to remedy them, at the time of the Sisters' visit; and if they cannot be immediately remedied, she shall keep a register of them apart, that they may be provided for in due time.

7. On the day of meeting of the Ladies and Sisters of Mercy, she shall lay before them a list of the cases which she was unable to relieve; and she shall propose them to these Ladies, that they may confer among themselves as to the most suitable means of giving relief.

8. In the same assemblies of the Ladies and Sisters of Mercy, she shall propose, in the the first place, the visiting of the sick, and see that some of the associated Ladies accompany the Sisters of St. Joseph, that these visits be made with effect and edification; secondly, that persons be chosen to collect money through the city, and, where such is the custom, at the doors of the churches; thirdly, that among other necessities, those of the imprisoned, of the hospital, of the orphans, of every other kind of distress be treated of in these meetings.

CHAPTER VIII.

RULES FOR THE CONDUCTRESS OF MERCY.

In all places where we have establishments, our Sisters shall take care to introduce the Confraternity of Mercy, unless there be already one established. In such case, they shall not interfere with it, unless they be requested to take charge of it.

This Confraternity consists of Ladies who are charitably disposed. They shall meet at stated times, at the house of the Sisters, at any hour that shall be deemed the most convenient to hold their conferences.

Besides this, they shall meet once a month, or more frequently if thought advisable, at which meeting all those associated shall attend; and the wants of the poor shall be proposed, and afterwards the means of succorring them shall be provided for.

The Superior herself, or a Sister whom she shall specially assign for this purpose, is to have the direction of this Confraternity; and the Sister to be appointed should be one of the most edifying and prudent in the whole Community, and shall observe the following rules in her office:

1. She shall often implore the light of the Holy Ghost, especially on the days of the meetings, that she may be able to instruct those whom she will have to address and direct.

2. She shall consult the Spiritual Father as to the manner of conducting the associated Ladies in a spiritual life. He shall indicate to her the books to be adopted for spiritual reading, which are to be suitable to persons of the various conditions of life.

3. She shall commence the meeting by a spiritual lecture; afterwards, she shall give the instructions and make such reproofs as she may deem necessary.

4. She shall make use of the Ladies of the Confraternity for correcting the evils, and for advancing the glory of God in the various parts of the town or parish; assigning to each one a particular duty to be performed; or a particular distress or scandal to redress or correct.

5. She shall conduct the married ladies to the perfection of their state, and also engage them to gain, by their mildness and prayers, their husbands to God; to educate their children in the love of God, and in the fear and hatred of sin; to instruct and correct their domestics, and, on no account, to permit any scandal in their families; and she shall draw them to watch over their entire neighborhood, so as to banish from it all evils, and to introduce, as much as possible, practises of piety.

6. She shall try to inspire widows with the spirit of patience and mortification; young ladies with a love of virtue, of innocence of

modesty, of piety, of decorum, together with a thorough aversion for vanity, and for everything that would, in any way, be contrary to purity of life. To domestics they shall inculcate the virtues of obedience, submismission, fidelity, patience and punctuality in their prayers.

7. She shall, in all the meetings, require the strict observance of the ceremonies and rules prescribed in the Directory, which the Bishop, or Spiritual Father, shall prescribe for the direction of this Confraternity.

CHAPTER IX.

RULES FOR THE PORTRESS.

1. The Portress should bear impressed on her countenance and deportment the image of the virtue which reigns among the Sisters of the Congregation of St. Joseph. Hence, she should study to edify all who call at the door of the Community, by her modesty, humility, mildness, patience and holy conversation, whenever she may be obliged to speak.

2. The door shall be locked at all times, and the Portress shall keep the key attached to her side, which she shall not give to any one without permission. At night, having locked all the doors, she shall deposit the keys with the Superior, who shall assign another Sister to keep company with her, when

it may be necessary to open the doors at night.

3. If the Sisters cannot have a Chapel at home for hearing Mass, they shall go out for this purpose at suitable hours. The Portress shall, in the mean time, keep the key till their return; at which time the Superior shall deliver the key of the door to be kept by another Sister whilst the Portress herself goes to Mass.

4. Besides the first door, in which there shall be a small window with a shutter, through which the persons knocking can be seen, but which door only opens with the permission of the Superior, there shall be another inner door, leading to the first or outer door, and of which the Portress shall keep the key. No persons shall go out without her permission; she alone shall keep the key, and shall lock the doors before nightfall.

5. Ladies alone are admissible to the house, and to the apartment in which the exercises of the Confraternity are held.

6. The Portress shall not call any **Sister,** or deliver any commission, without **the** permission of the Superior. And if any letters, or parcels, be left for any of the Community, she shall present them to the Superior, before any Sister receive them.

7. When it be necessary to admit the **Vicar-General,** the Physician, Apothecary, **or others,** there shall always be two Sisters **to conduct**

them to the place where they are going; and the Portress shall not open the first door till the two Sisters be ready to receive them.

8. If any one call to speak to the Portress, she shall direct the person to the place destined for strangers, then ask the permission of the Superior, and beg of her to send some Sister in her place to answer the door.

9. What has been said in this Chapter shall be observed in all the houses belonging to the Congregation; but in hospitals, the houses of the poor, and where there may not be all the conveniences that might be desired, the Superiors of such establishments shall observe, and cause to be observed by the Portress, the spirit of these rules, as far as may be practicable.

10. The Portress shall be exact in informing the Superior of all things which she may observe, contrary to good example or the Constitutions.

CHAPTER X.

RULES FOR THE OTHER OFFICERS.

Many other Officers are employed in the houses of the Congregation; for example, the Cook, the Infirmarian, Sacristan, and others. It is not necessary to prescribe for them any particular rules; it is sufficient for them to observe the following general directions:

3. They **shall attend** to the orders of the Superior with great exactness, and endeavor to discharge them with great purity of intention, humility, devotion; seeking alone, in all things, the greater glory of God and the welfare of the Community.

2. Let them observe in their various offices, as far as possible, great order, cleanliness and decorum.

3. Let them perform all things with exactness and diligence, without precipitation; but with such evenness of mind, that they may be enabled to raise their souls to God, and keep themselves always in His presence.

4. Let them not undertake charges which are above their capacities: nor yield to agitation nor over anxiety, under the pretext of obedience and charity. Let them respectfully represent to the Superior what they can perform, taking care not to flatter themselves; and then let them submit to whatever the Superior may order, having great confidence in God, who will assist them.

CHAPTER XI.

OF THE APPOINTMENT OF OFFICERS.

The Bishop shall name the Superior in those houses where there are not six professed Sisters in the Community. He can also name the Superior in houses where the Sisters are even very numerous, or he can have them chosen by the Chapter of Sisters. He can also choose a Sister of a different house and diocese, and name her Superior. Although Superiors ought not, ordinarily, to continue in office beyond the term of three years, nevertheless, he can confirm them in office for whatever number of years he may deem fit. When the Superiors do not acquit themselves well of their charge, or for other reasons, he can depose them, change them, and name others in their place. He can exercise the same power in respect to the Assistant and the other officers, for all are under his authority.

The Spiritual Father shall have the same power, excepting that he cannot name, or depose, or change from one house to another any Superior, without the approbation of the Bishop. Each Superior, at the termination of the three years, shall give notice of the fact, to the Bishop, or to the Spiritual Father, and if confirmed in her office for a longer time, she shall continue as in the preceding years. If they desire that the Community elect another, the election shall take place according to what is laid down in the following chapter.

CHAPTER XII.

OF THE ELECTION OF THE SUPERIOR.

The elections can be at any time the Bishop

may desire; nevertheless, they shall generally take place on the Tuesday after the Feast of the Ascension, according to the example of the Sisters of the Visitation; which is also the day on which the Apostles elected St. Matthias in place of Judas Iscariot. The Bishop, or Spiritual Father, will preside at these elections; but in case they should not, they will depute some prudent and enlightened priest to do so in their place.

On Saturday after the Feast of Ascension, the person who is to preside shall assemble the Sisters, both Professed and Novices, in the Chapel of the house, or in some room, if there be no Chapel, and being seated before the altar, and the Sisters standing up, being ranged, some on one side, others on the other, the Superior in the midst of them, on bended knees, shall renounce the office of Superior, resigning it into the hands of the said President; and she shall then accuse herself of the faults committed in her office, and the President shall accept her demission, saying: "The Congregation exonerates you, in the Name of the Father, and of the Son, and of the Holy Ghost." He will then enjoin a penance on her, and shall give the charge of the house to the Assistant; and the late Superior shall retire, and take her place according to the time of her profession.

The President shall then give notice to the Sisters of the election of a new Superior, which is to take place on the following Tuesday; and shall admonish them to reflect on the matter most seriously, and to propose to themselves no other consideration but the greater glory of God. Then the Hymn, "*Veni Creator Spiritus,*" is to be sung, with its prayer; after which all retire.

The following Sunday, all the Sisters shall offer up the Holy Communion to obtain of the Almighty the grace of making an election according to His Divine Will; and every day the above Hymn, "*Veni Creator Spiritus,*" with the prayer to the Holy Ghost, will be said for the same intention. In the meantime the Sisters will not speak of the election which is to take place; but each one shall seriously think on what she should do, according to the views of God.

On the following Tuesday, all the Sisters shall offer up their Communion for the above purpose; after which the person who is to preside will assemble them in the Chapel, where all, on bended knees, shall say the Hymn, "*Veni Creator Spiritus,*" with the prayer of the Holy Ghost. Then the President shall exhort them to give their votes to the person whom they think most worthy of being Superior. They then shall name a **Secretary** of the Chapter.

Afterwards, the Assistant shall **go to the**

Secretary, who shall be seated at a table in the extremity of the Chapel, and on the table there shall be a quantity of small pieces of blank paper, with ink and pens and sand. The Assistant shall ask her in a low voice, to write the name of two or three Sisters, as she may think proper, on two or three pieces of paper. Having got these names in writing, she shall fold them up that no one may be able to see them, and she shall return to her place.

All the Sisters shall go in succession, according to their rank to obtain the names of at least two Sisters written on pieces of paper, in like manner as the Assistant did.

If any Sister be sick, the President, with a Counsellor and the Secretary, shall go to obtain her vote. She shall name in a low voice to the Secretary, two Sisters' names, to be written on small pieces of paper, and and shall hand to the President the ticket she pleases, which he shall take to the Chapter.

When all the Sisters shall have taken tickets, the Assistant shall first go with one of the tickets and place it in a box, which shall be on the altar. All the others shall in like manner, according to their rank, drop their ticket in the box, and the President shall put there the tickets of the sick, if there be any.

When all the tickets are put in the box

the President, accompanied by the two Counsellors, and in their presence, shall count them, to ascertain if the proper number of tickets be in the box. He shall afterwards open them; and the Sister who shall have the greater number of votes, shall be the Superior.

The President shall declare in a loud voice the name of her who has been elected. She shall immediately kneel down before the altar, make her profession of faith; and the President shall confirm the election saying: "By the authority which we have we confirm your election, that you be Superior of this house and Community of the daughters of St. Joseph: in the Name of the Father, and of the Son, and of the Holy Ghost." She shall humbly accept the charge, without either excusing herself, or refusing it.

She shall then occupy the place of Superior; and all the Sisters, one after another, shall go to kiss her hand on bended knees; after which the Chapter is terminated by the "*Te Deum Laudamus.*" Afterwards the Assistant shall record in a book the day of the election.

Should the votes be equally divided between two or three Sisters, these shall draw lots. The younger shall draw first, and the one who shall draw the ticket on which the word "*Superior*" shall be written, shall be confirmed by the President as the Superior, and the Sisters shall acknowledge her in the manner above laid down.

No Sister shall be eligible to be Superior who has not been five years professed, and who is not thirty years of age; unless there be none of that age, or that a younger Sister has been found more suitable to be Superior. But, in all cases, the Sisters should never elect a person to be Superior, whom they, in conscience, do not judge to be fit to fulfill the the duties of that office, as laid down in the First Chapter of this Part, where her rules and her qualifications are specified. The Sisters should, therefore, read and examine well that Chapter, to regulate them in the election they are about to make.

The Superior, when elected, shall make choice of an Assistant and Co-adjutrix, according to the views of God, and shall propose them in Chapter to the Sisters, and their election shall be declared by the plurality of voices. If they have not a plurality of votes, she shall propose the names of others, and their election shall be conducted as that for a Superior.

In the Chapter of *Election of Officers*, the Sisters can re-elect the Superior, Assistants, Co-adjutrixes, as often as they deem proper for the welfare of the Community. In regard to the other officers, the Superior, with the advice of the Assistant, Co-adjutrix, and Counsellors, can name them, and change them as she shall think most advisable. She can also confer many offices on the same Sister, where the Community is limited in number, and the offices are not so embarrassing but that one Sister may easily discharge them.

In small Communities, where there are only four or five Sisters, there shall be no Assistant, but, in the absence of the Superior, the senior Sister shall govern the house; unless the Bishop, or Spiritual Father, name another more suitable to govern. And the Superior shall have, moreover, the power to entrust all the offices to the Sister she shall consider most fit.

CHAPTER XIII.

OF THE RULES APPLICABLE TO ALL THE SISTERS.

1. All the Sisters should entertain great esteem and love for their vocation, considering that God has called them, and has bestowed on them the most suitable means of advancing His own glory, and their own sanctification. If, at any time, they should experience any disgust for it, or should feel greater esteem or attachment for other vocations, they should promptly renounce such suggestions as temptations, persuading themselves that God wishes them where they are, and nowhere else.

2. **They shall** entertain **great respect,** love and confidence towards their Superiors. They shall honor Jesus Christ in them; they shall salute them with reverence in meeting them, and always address them with mildness and respect. They shall love them as their mothers, and manifest to them all their troubles of mind, and interior feelings; and have recourse to them in all their spiritual and corporal wants.

3. They shall prefer the general to a particular good, so as to yield up willingly their own satisfaction and interest, when there is question of accomodating each other, or rendering a service to the community, or even to an individual Sister.

4. They shall demean **themselves** with great moderation, so that in their gait, words, looks and actions they may on all occasions show forth the virtues of true religious, and edify one another and all who may see them. They shall not perform their duties with precipitation, over-anxiety, confusion, or noise, and shall always preserve themselves in the presence of God.

5. They shall write no letter, nor receive any without the permission of the Superior, who shall read them, or open them if she think proper.

5. They shall take their meals with great decorum, and in the large Communities each **Sister** shall have her **portion,** and in the

smaller ones, the Superior shall arrange matters as they find most convenient. One or more of the Sisters shall read during the repasts in the large Communities; in the smaller ones, there shall be reading at least at the commencement, during which the Sisters shall observe strict silence.

7. After meals they shall assemble together for recreation, entertaining one another in things that are innocent and agreeable. They should neither speak of worldly news, which distracts the mind; they should also avoid loud laughter and unbecoming demeanor, bearing in mind the words of St. Paul: "Rejoice in the Lord always; again I say rejoice. Let your modesty be known to all men. The Lord is nigh."*

8. Each Sister shall sweep her own room every day; and besides, shall sweep the places assigned to her by the Superior or Assistant. Great diligence shall be observed by the Sisters in these particulars, that all persons may be edified by the good order and cleanliness of the establishment.

9. The Sisters are not to remain beyond half an hour in conversation with strangers, without the permission of the Superior, who ought not to give leave for long conversations, unless there be some real necessity therefor.

---
* Philip, 4.

10. They are not to read profane books, nor even new books of devotion, without permission of the Spiritual Father, or of the Confessor.

11. No Sister shall ever go out of the house without another Sister to accompany her, or at least some person of the house; so that they shall be always with some one, unless in some very extraordinary and inevitable case of necessity. When abroad, they shall walk with great modesty, with downcast eyes, and are not to separate from one another. They are never to sleep out of a house of the Congregation, without the permission of the Superior, who shall not grant it unless in a case of most urgent necessity.

12. They can take a walk in the suburbs of the town once a week; they should be two by two or in fours, but they should never choose those places that are much resorted to by the world.

13. When a Sister is obliged, by business, to go on a journey, the Superior shall provide her with the conveniences for the purpose, as money, etc.; and she shall send a Sister with her, or some very faithful woman to accompany her.

14. Sisters can, with the permission of the Superiors, visit other houses of the Congregation; but it will be necessary to have the written permission of their Superiors. If any should present herself at any house without

such permission in writing, the Superior shall immediately acquaint the Spiritual Father of it, and he shall cause her to be punished, and to be sent back to her house without delay.

15. If a Sister should be obliged to go into another diocese, she must have the permission of the Bishop, in writing, or of the Spiritual Father, that it may appear that she travels under obedience.

16. We order all Superiors of our houses to receive most charitably all Sisters of the Congregation, who travel and have their permission in due form. They, and all the Sisters, shall salute them and treat them most affectionately and hospitably, according to the means of their establishment, without exacting anything for their expenses.

17. We order all Sisters, in any journey they may make, to lodge in the houses of the Congregation they may meet with; and we forbid them to remain elsewhere, not even in the house of their father, without the permission of the Superior of the place; which permission is not to be granted, except for most urgent reasons, and with the advice of the Counsellors.

The other general rules are contained in the different **Chapters of these Constitutions**

Directions for Sisters Employed in the Schools

CHAPTER I.

OF THE DIRECTRESS OF THE SCHOOL.

The Directress of the Academy is intrusted with the management of all things relating to the young ladies confided to her care: so that, whilst making continual progress in science, and the accomplishments suited to their sex, they may also constantly advance in piety and virtue.

She shall endeavor to edify all with whom she may have to treat, in the discharge of the duties of her office, by her example and conduct, and the practice of every virtue. She should exhibit, on all occasions, great humility and charity toward the Sisters who assist her in the Academy, and respect and submission toward the Superior.

She shall exercise a constant vigilance in regard to the pupils, and maintain good order and discipline in the school; she shall watch with a special care over them, and do all in her power to promote their advancement in piety and learning. She shall inculcate in them the love and practice of Christian modesty, the brightest ornament of female youth, and she shall see that they read no book of dangerous tendency

She shall examine the pupils placed at the Academy, and place them in the classes suited to their capacity and advancement.

She shall take care that the pupils be never left alone, but that they be constantly under the guardianship of Monitresses, when not in class.

She shall carefully apply herself to make the pupils practice the rules of Christian politeness, not to teach the love of pleasure and dress, but how to make themselves esteemed in society. She shall reform in them all that appears reprehensible in their manners, and shall teach them how to salute, interrogate, answer, etc., much more by practice than by explanation, contenting herself to correct them, according as they shall have committed faults against politeness.

Finally, the Directress should frequently reflect on the importance of the trust confided to her care; she should consider how guilty she would render herself before God in abusing that trust, either by an excessive harshness or severity, or by too great indulgence or culpable negligence in the exercises of her office; and, on the other hand, she should endeavor to excite herself to a **great** confidence in God, and an ardent zeal to advance His glory in the faithful discharge of the duties imposed on her.

CHAPTER II.

RULES FOR THE SISTER TEACHER.

The Sisters of St. Joseph being particularly called by the Rt. Rev. Bishop and Rev. Superior to give to children a Christian education, shall make it their principal care to teach them the morning and evening prayer and the catechism.

They shall likewise apply themselves with much zeal to procure them the necessary science for life; such as reading, writing, orthography, grammar and arithmetic. They shall also teach history, geography and plain sewing to children that shall be sufficiently advanced in the other branches of instruction.

It enters into the duties of the Sisters of the parochial schools to form their pupils to politeness; it seems even that, after religion, there is nothing of greater importance.

The Sisters shall then reform in their pupils all that shall appear reprehensible in their manners, and shall teach them the respect due to their parents, and persons with whom they shall have any correspondence, etc.

They shall take care that the scholars always keep themselves neat and clean; they shall exact of them to have their hair combed, their faces and hands washed before entering school.

The Sisters shall not inflict corporal punishment on the children intrusted to their care; if a child prove incorrigible, after suitable chastisement shall have been given, she shall be dismissed with the concurrence of the Superior, and after the parents shall have been acquainted.

Of all the penances that a Sister can give, that of *task* is the most suitable for them, and the least disagreeable to parents. It is the most suitable for a Sister in this, that all harshness, all that appears too much like correction, is a thing as humbling for her who gives it as for her who receives it; for, to strike a child for a fault of small consequence, is to resist the sentiments of humanity to which this kind of chastisement is repugnant.

PART V.

Of the Spiritual Exercises to be Practised by the Sisters.

In this Fifth Part, we shall lay down the exercises to be adopted in our Congregation; and to do so with order, we shall divide them according to the time they are practised; namely: annual, monthly, weekly, and daily exercises. We shall add the distribution of the hours of each day, or the *orarium*.

CHAPTER I.

OF THE ANNUAL EXERCISES.

1. At the beginning of the year, the Sisters shall ask their Director or Superior to assign them a Saint to be their protector during the year.

2. Preparatory to the Feasts of the Visitation and Conception of the most Blessed Virgin Mary, and the Feast of St. Joseph, the Sisters shall dispose themselves for the celebration of them, by three days of more than

ordinary recollection. They shall give half an hour additional to prayer; observe silence, except in time of recreation; not speaking without necessity. The three days' devotion, called *Triduum*, before the Feast of the Visitation, shall be offered by the Sisters to obtain of Jesus, through the intercession of His Virgin Mother Mary, that He may visit and sanctify their Congregation, as He sanctified John the Baptist, while still in the womb of his mother; and that He may animate them in visiting the sick and poor, with the same zeal with which Mary was animated in visiting St. Elizabeth. They shall offer the *Triduum* before the Feast of the Conception, to beg of Mary to obtain for them of her Divine Son the grace of conceiving great designs for their own sanctification and the welfare of their neighbor; and great purity of intention in all their actions and whole conduct. The *Triduum* before the Feast of St. Joseph is to obtain of their Glorious Patriarch the continuance of his holy protection, and the advancements of their Congregation in all virtues.

3. They shall renew their vows on the Feast of the Visitation of the most Blessed Virgin, in presence of the Bishop, or of their Spiritual Father, or of their Director, immediately before receiving the most Holy Communion at his hand saying: "My God, I renew my vows of poverty, chastity, and

obedience, hoping with thy Divine grace, to observe them faithfully all my life."

4. They shall perform a retreat of eight or ten days, every year; and, if it be possible, they shall begin it on the Feast of the Ascension and finish it at Penticost, unless the Superior may deem another time more suitable. —The various exercises of the retreat shall be pointed out to them by their Spiritual Director, or by the Superior. We ordain that all the Sisters perform the Spiritual Retreat each year, with an inviolable exactness, as being most essential for their advancement in the perfection to which they are called.

5. The Sisters who may not be in their spiritual retreat during the ten days before Penticost, shall perform half an hour's additional devotions on those days, to dispose themselves for the reception of the Holy Ghost, who is the principle of all the graces and virtues necessary for their salvation.

6. From Monday in Holy Week to the following Wednesday, they shall retrench half their recreation; and from Holy Thursday to Holy Saturday, they shall dispense entirely with recreation, in order that they may apply their minds with more affection and sorrow to contemplate the Passion and Death of our Saviour.

7. Eight days previous to the principal Feasts, they shall converse on the means of passing them most usefully and most de-

voutly; and on the vigils of the said Feasts, they shall deprive themselves of the usual recreation.

8. They shall make an annual confession, towards the end of each year, unless they had made it at the time of spiritual retreat.

CHAPTER II.

OF THE EXERCISES OF EACH MONTH.

1. On the first day of each month, the Sisters shall go to Holy Communion, for which they shall prepare by half a quarter of an hour of additional prayer to obtain the grace of passing that month with renewed fervor. After returning thanks, they shall make the acts, as found at the end of the Directory.

2. On the first Sunday of each month, they shall offer a Communion for all their Superiors; and, if unable on that day, they shall do so as soon as convenient, and on the same day they shall say a third part of the Rosary for the same intention.

3. At the commencement of the month, the Sisters shall, in pairs, agree to practise some virtue, or correct themselves of some fault to which they may be subject; with the obligation of mildly admonishing each other in case of necessity, in regard to this resolution. The person admonished shall say the hymn, "*Veni Creator Spiritus,*" for

the Sister who corrected her. This practise is observed with great fruit in the Convents of the Visitation.

4. On the first or last day of the month, the Sisters shall draw tickets for the name of a Saint, whom, during the month, they shall invoke with special confidence; they shall go to Communion in his honor, and practise the virtue marked on the ticket. The Superior shall have, for this purpose, tickets with the name of the Saint of each day, printed or written, with the name of some particular virtue. Having said the "*Veni Creator Spiritus*" together, the Superior shall present them, that each Sister may draw one.

5. At the end of the month they shall take a review of all the graces received from God, and most humbly return Him thanks for them, and also of the principal faults committed during the same time, and acknowledge them with great humility, without scruple or embarrassment, in order more perfectly to purify their souls.

CHAPTER III.

OF THE EXERCISES OF EACH WEEK.

1. On Sundays and Festivals the Sisters shall recite together the Little Office of Our Lady, in their Chapel or Oratory, in a reverent, distinct and intelligent manner. They

shall also assist, when able, at the parochial Mass, and at Vespers; as also at the sermons and instructions, leaving in the house such Sisters as are necessary to guard it and attend to any duty.

2. They shall go to confession once a week.

3. They shall approach the Holy Communion on all Sundays and Feasts of the year; and on Thursdays, if Wednesday or Friday be not Festival days. They may also receive Communion on the other days, by turns, one after another; but these Communions and all others are to be made only with the permission of the Superior, who can withhold her permission, as she thinks proper, and such privation is to be recieved with humility.

4. They shall fast on all Saturdays, and exercise the discipline on themselves during the recital of the *"Hail Holy Queen,"* and the psalm, *"From the Depths I have Cried to Thee, O Lord,"* which they shall recite together.

5. They shall hold a Chapter every Friday, and a Conference on all Sundays, if possible.

CHAPTER IV.

THE EXERCISES OF EACH DAY.

1. The Sisters shall say every day the Litanies of the Holy Name of Jesus, of the

Blessed Virgin Mary, of St. Joseph, and of All Saints.

2. They shall make a meditation twice a day; in the morning and after dinner.

3. They shall say a third part of the Rosary of the Virgin Mary, and the devotion called the Crown of Mary, consisting of three *Paters* or *Our Fathers*, and twelve *Aves* or *Hail Marys*.

4. They shall also hear Mass, and make a spiritual lecture.

5. On every day they shall say together the Little Office of the Holy Ghost, in their Chapel. They will perform these exercises at the hours marked in the following Chapter.

CHAPTER V.

THE DISTRIBUTION OF TIME, OR ORARIUM, FOR THE EXERCISES OF THE DAY.

The Sisters shall rise at five o'clock in the summer, and in winter at six. In rising, they shall offer their hearts to God, and when dressed, they shall say morning prayers, the *Angelus* and the *Veni Creator*. They shall then make their meditation of half an hour, and end it by saying the *Pater*, *Ave* and *Gloria Patri*. After which they shall recite the Office of the Holy Ghost as far as Vespers, the Litanies of the holy name of Jesus, and one *Pater*, *Ave* and *Gloria Patri*, in honor of the Saint of the month.

Then each Sister shall attend to her work, during which she shall examine how she performed her meditation and other prayers.

They shall take breakfast at half-past seven o'clock, and about eight they shall hear Mass; and if they have received Communion, they shall remain a quarter of an hour longer. When returned from Mass they shall resume their work. At eleven o'clock they shall examine their conscience during a half-quarter of an hour, and then go to dinner, during which they shall have spiritual reading. There shall be an hour's recreation after dinner, which may, or may not, be passed in some light work, as the Superior may deem proper.

After recreation, they shall resume their work, until half-past twelve, at which time they shall say the Angelus, the *De profundis*," or "*From the Depths I cried to Thee O Lord*," the Litany of the Blessed Virgin, the prayer of St. Joseph, and a *Pater*, *Ave*, and *Gloria Patri*, for their benefactors. They shall then attend to their work in silence till one o'clock.

At one o'clock they shall say the *Veni Creator*, read a spiritual lecture for a quarter of an hour, and reflect on it till two o'clock.

At two o'clock some of the Sisters can go to visit the poor, and the remainder shall attend to their work.

At four o'clock they shall assemble to say

Vespers and Complin of the Holy Ghost, the Litany of St. Joseph, and a *Pater* and *Ave* for those who are in their agony. After which they shall perform half an hour's meditation; and terminate it by saying one *Pater* and *Ave*, a third part of the Rosary, the Crown of our Blessed Lady. Afterwards silence will be observed till six o'clock.

At six o'clock they shall go to supper, during which there shall be spiritual reading, and after it there shall be an hour's recreation. Then the Sisters shall go to their work, till a quarter past nine o'clock. At which hour they shall say the Litany of All Saints, as far as the words *Propitius este*, or *Be merciful to us*. They shall then examine their conscience, say the Litany of Our Lady, and read the meditation for the following morning. They shall afterwards retire in silence to rest, and not remain up beyond a quarter of an hour. They shall observe silence till after the next morning's meditation. On fast days, dinner shall be at half-past eleven o'clock, spiritual lecture at two, and collation at half-past six o'clock.

They shall say their prayers and other exercises of devotion in their Chapel or Oratory. On Sundays and Festivals, they shall say the Office of Our Lady, in place of the Office of the Holy Ghost.

PART VI.

Of the Means of Sustaining and Advancing the Congregation.

Having laid down the most essential rules for the perfection of our Congregation, it is now necessary to guard against certain defects which occasion relaxation in religious orders, and ultimately cause their destruction.

First, the reception of subjects without a real vocation, who have not the requisite qualifications, and who have not received proper training during the Novitiate. Second, ambition in seeking for offices. Third, the defective choice of Superiors. Fourth, the improper use made of authority by Superiors. Fifth, the neglect on the part of the Superiors to watch over and correct the faults of the Sisters. Sixth, the deficiency or excess in temporal matters. Seventh, indolence and the want of union. Eighth, too great intercourse with persons out of doors. Ninth, the multiplicity of Directors. Tenth, ignorance of the Constitutions and rules of the Institute; and negligence in reading and studying them.

CHAPTER I.

OF THE MEANS OF RECEIVING NONE BUT GOOD SUBJECTS INTO THE CONGREGATION.

The Sisters should bear in mind that in conscience they are bound to love the Congregation, and prefer its interests and its advancement to everything else; they should love it more than themselves, more than their parents or friends.

Hence, they should examine the candidates and Novices with extreme exactness. They cannot give their votes to persons with whom they are not acquainted, and whose qualifications, consequently, are not known to them. They should not rely on the account of others, where they have to pronounce judgment and give their vote.

When they shall have known the qualifications of those who present themselves, either to be received or professed, they shall in no case whatever vote for them unless they possess the qualifications required in the Third Part of these Constitutions. If they act otherwise, they become guilty of sin; and will have to answer before the tribunal of God for all the disorder and ruin that the persons thus received by them shall cause to the Congregation.

Above all things, the Sisters should never receive a subject who once left the Congregation, unless the Bishop, for weighty reasons, thought it proper to receive her.

It is not sufficient to use great circumspection in the reception of subjects. When persons are deemed suitable for the Congregation, and admitted to their probation, the Superior and the Mistresses of the Novices should have special care of their education and training to a spiritual life, by following punctually the rules laid down in the Third Part, in the Chapter *"For the Education of Novices,"* and in the Fourth Part, in the Chapter *"Regarding the Mistress of Novices."*

Should a Superior or Mistress of Novices neglect to discharge her duty faithfully, or suffer herself to be deceived or prepossessed in favor of a Candidate or Novice who had not the requisite qualifications, the Sisters aware of the circumstance should inform the Bishop or Spiritual Father thereof.

CHAPTER II.

OF THE MEANS OF DESTROYING AMBITION.

Ambition being the daughter of pride, is equally criminal. It precipitated Lucifer from Heaven into the abyss of hell; it caused Adam to fall from the state of grace and innocence, and cast him and his posterity into so many temporal and eternal evils, whose woful consequences are so sensibly experienced; it is the source of all our sins; in fine, it caused Jesus Christ to suffer so much and to die in an ignominious manner on the cross.

This truth, well weighed and meditated on, ought not only prevent our Sisters from ambitioning the office of Superior; but should even impress them with a lively horror for this vice.

If they consider, moreover, that those who enter on an office with an ambitious spirit, can neither please God, nor work out their own salvation : "For God resists the proud and giveth His grace to the humble ;" * and if they reflect that though God in His excessive mercy may grant them the light necessary to conduct others, still they will not obtain the graces requisite for their own sanctification, because pride, which fills their mind with ambitious views, will work their ruin, though they may conduct others in the road of salvation.

Were Sisters well impressed with these truths, they would not ambition office, and, consequently, feel no party spirit, nor allow themselves to be influenced by those who are disposed to factious conduct, in order to attain any office.

If, however, a Sister be convicted of having, either directly or indirectly, endeavored to attain the office of Superior, or any other charge, she shall be deprived of it for

---

* St. Peter, v. 5.

her whole life; neither can she be dispensed from this disqualification, or rendered eligible for at least ten years, even though she were to give evidences of humility; except in the case when the Bishop, or, with his consent, the Spiritual Father, were to grant a dispensation.

If a Superior, or Assistant, or others in office, be discovered to have canvassed for any charge, she shall be at once deposed, and have suitable penance imposed on her by the Bishop or Spiritual Father.

Some days prior to the election of officers, the Superior shall call a Chapter of all the Sisters, and command them, under obedience, to renounce any Sister who may have canvassed for any office, in order that she be excluded from the election as unworthy.

CHAPTER III.

OF THE MEANS OF AVOIDING A BAD CHOICE OF SUPERIORS.

A bad choice of Superiors may proceed, either from malice, when a person voluntarily chooses those who are known to be unworthy; or from ignorance, when a person does not know what are the qualifications requisite in a Superior.

To remedy the first evil, the person who shall preside at the Chapter for election shall command all the Sisters to give their votes to the persons they conscientiously believe most worthy; and all shall protest that they will do so. Should they give votes in favor of persons whom they believe unworthy, they commit a mortal sin, and will have to answer, at the tribunal of God, for all evil consequences which the Congregation, or any Sister, may sustain from the bad conduct of Superiors for whom they may have voted.

To remedy the second evil, the Sisters should read attentively in Part Four of these Constitutions, the rules regarding Superiors and other officers; where they can clearly see the qualifications requisite for them to discharge in a proper manner their respective duties. They will, then, with the grace of God, be enabled to discern what Sisters are most worthy and capable, and vote accordingly for those Sisters.

CHAPTER IV.

OF THE MEANS OF PREVENTING SUPERIORS MAKING AN UNDUE USE OF THEIR AUTHORITY.

Superiors who are not well founded in humility, and who do not bear in mind that they are appointed only to serve the other Sisters, easily yield to pride; and in the place of using their authority with fear, they employ it to satisfy their own private ends, to the great prejudice of the general and special welfare of the Community.

To check this excessive liberty, and to limit the authority of Superiors in matters of importance, either in the conduct of the Sisters, or in the government of the house, she shall do nothing without her Counsellors; and she shall follow the majority of votes, unless it clearly appears that her opinion is preferable. In this latter case, if the Spiritual Father agree in sentiment with her, she may differ from her Counsellors, and act according to her own opinion. Secondly, if a Superior commit any great fault, which may God forbid, the Spiritual Father shall have power to depose her, and appoint another in her place. Thirdly, the Superior shall declare her faults every Holy Thursday, in presence of the Sisters, and the Admonitrix shall admonish her, in case there be any complaints made of her government.

CHAPTER V.

OF THE MEANS OF PREVENTING NEGLIGENCE ON THE PART OF THE SUPERIOR IN WATCHING OVER AND CORRECTING THE SISTERS.

The neglect of Superiors to watch over the interests of the Community, and correct what may be wrong, arises either from a want of zeal for the spiritual advancement of all, or from a too great solicitude for the temporal concerns of their house, or perhaps from meddling with secular affairs.

Superiors should remember the terrible account they must render to God; first, of all the good they neglected to do for those under their care, by means of good example, seasonable advice; secondly, of all the evil and disorder they tolerated in the house, through human respect, or want of zeal. They should, therefore, constantly beg of God renewed fervor in laboring for the greater perfection of all; and still more, they should endeavor to become models of exact observance of all the rules.

The Monitors and Counsellors should also take care to correct whatever they see faulty, but always with great sweetness of manner. They should animate all, by word and example, to zeal for the spiritual advancement of the Institute. They should suggest to all the Sisters to offer a Communion, once every month, and the Rosary once every week, to obtain an increase of light and fervor of the Holy Ghost.

To prevent the embarrassments and distractions arising from temporal concerns from interfering with the spiritual care of the Community, Superiors should reflect that it is the intention of the Institute that they specially apply themselves to conduct those subject to them to perfection, and maintain them in peace and perfect observ nce of the rules. With respect to the temporal affairs, they should make choice of good officers; see that they discharge their duties faithfully; and require an account from them of their duties. As to secular affairs, they should not interefere in them, unless the orders of Superiors, absolute necessity, or pressing cases of charity oblige them to it. They shall excuse themselves from attending to such affairs as are incompatible with their state, and their present duties, in a kindly and affable manner, and remember that it is better to leave all worldly affairs perish, than that one soul be lost.

The Constitutions afford two means of avoiding negligence on the part of Superiors, as it is required that they should hold Conferences and Chapters for the purpose of instructing and correcting the Sisters. We shall explain them in the following Chapters.

CHAPTER VI.

OF CONFERENCES.

The Superior shall assemble all the Sisters, on Sunday evenings, after recreation, and she shall commence the Conference by proposing to them what she may judge proper for the spiritual or temporal welfare of the house, or of the Congregation in general, or any particular Sister. She shall, on these occasions, speak of the defects of the house, of the non-observance of rule, or of the relaxation on any particular point. She shall take the advice of the Sisters on such things as may demand amendment.

They shall answer with great respect, simplicity and sincerity, saying what God may inspire them with. They shall give their opinions, one after another, without hurry or disregard for one another, avoiding all obstinacy and precipitation. Each one should advance what she deems for the welfare of the Congregation, or of the house, or of individuals.

When all have given their opinions, the Superior shall terminate the Conference; concluding, from what has been said, what she judges most advantageous, and all shall adhere to what has been thus resolved on.

CHAPTER VII.

OF THE CHAPTER OF FAULTS.

Besides the Chapters assembled by the Superior for the election of officers, for the admission of subjects, for the profession of Novices, and other important matters, in which all the Sisters shall give their vote, except relatives in the first degree, and where only the senior or that one who is highest in rank shall vote,

The Superior of each house shall assemble

the Sisters in Chapter, every Friday, either after the Office, or after the recreation, in the evening, at which all Sisters, both professed and non-professed, shall assist, except those who may be sick.

The Superior and Sisters being assembled, and ranged according to their rank and seniority, the Superior shall begin by the Hymn of the Holy Ghost, *Veni Creator*, and the prayer. She shall then read and explain some Chapter of the Constitutions, or a Chapter out of a pious book, according as the Superior may deem most advisable. Should she perfer to say a few words to them, she can also adopt this method.

The lecture being terminated, the Superior shall say: "*Sit Nomen Domini Benedictum*" — '*May the Name of the Lord be praised.*" Then all the Sisters shall kneel down, and the first shall kiss the ground, and declare her faults,—accusing herself of some one in particular; she shall humbly listen to what shall be said to her for her correction, and shall accept the penance imposed on her; after which she shall kiss the ground, and remain on her knees till all have declared their faults in the same manner.

All having finished, the Superior shall rise from her seat, and say: "*Let us bless the Lord;*" and the Sisters shall rise from their knees, and answer; "*Thanks be to God;*" and they shall all leave the Chapter in silence.

If there should be any lay Sisters, they shall first kneel down and declare their faults, and after these, the Novices shall kneel down and declare their faults; and having received from the Superior correction and penance, they shall leave the Chapter-room on intimation given to them.—When these have left the room, the Professed Sisters, who remained sitting, shall declare their faults in the order above mentioned.

The Sisters shall listen with great attention and profound respect to what the Superior may say for their instruction and correction. They are strictly forbidden to contradict what may be said to them, or to excuse themselves, unless the Superior allow them to give an explanation. If any Sister act otherwise, the Superior shall immediately impose silence on her; and if she do not obey, she shall be punished according to her fault.

When Sisters declare their faults, they shall only accuse themselves of exterior faults; as, for example, having omitted their prayers, violated silence, and other observances of rules; having spoken angrily, committed impatiences, spoken against charity or in too loud a tone; having told lies, answered disrespectfully, refused a kindness, despised advice, neglected the duties of their employment, and such like. As to their interior faults, they shall reserve them for their confessor, or for their private communications with the Superior, to whom they can open their interior, in order to obtain the lights necessary for their amendment and progress in virtue.

The Sisters should remember that the Chapter is an image of the last judgment, where all our faults will be manifested; with this difference, that the manifestation of our faults made in the Chapter acquires for us the remission at least of our venial faults, the augmentation of grace, and the deliverance from the pains of purgatory, provided it be made with humility and contrition, and that the corrections and penances imposed be received with humility. In this spirit the Sisters should go to the Chapter, and on no account should they, on leaving it, murmur or complain on account of anything said on the occasion by the Superior.

The Superior can, with prudence, impose such penances as are proportioned to the faults of the Sisters; as certain prayers, pious lectures, meditation, silence, kissing the ground, loss or abridgment of recreation, or of a part of a meal, or of Communion; to eat on the ground, kiss the feet of the Sisters, take the discipline, to fast, to depose from office for some days, or forever, to remain in one's room, or other such punishments as the Superior may deem suitable.

CHAPTER VIII.

OF THE MEANS OF AVOIDING EITHER DEFICIENCY OR EXCESS OF TEMPORAL GOODS.

Experience shows that a deficiency or excess of temporal goods often cause inobservance of rules and disorder in religious communities. To guard against such evils—

1. The Bishop or the Spiritual Father will please not to allow one of the houses of our Congregation to be established where there is not support for at least three Sisters, as in no case can less than three Sisters be in any establishment. The Superiors of houses shall always oppose the introduction of more Sisters into an establishment than the means of support allow. The Sisters shall also be assiduous in labor, bearing in mind the words of St. Paul: "If any one will not work, neither let him eat. We have heard there are some among you who walk disorderly, working not at all, but curiously meddling."*

2. To avoid any excess of property, we require that whatever surplus remain after the moderate support of the Sisters and of the establishment, be employed partly for the poor, and partly in providing Church ornaments for the Sisters' Oratory, and for

---

* 2 Thes. 3.

other poor neighboring Churches. When Superiors visit our houses, having certified the accounts they shall please to apply whatever surplus remains in any of them to the above specified purposes.

CHAPTER IX.

OF THE MEANS OF AVOIDING IDLENESS AND DISUNION.

Useless actions, as well as useless words, are a subject of condemnation, as Christ warns us; hence the Sisters shall avoid all loss of time, bearing in mind the words of St. Paul, "Whilst we have time, let us work good to all men." *

The Superior shall specially take care to cause all the Sisters to observe most strictly what is prescribed in the last Chapter of Part V., regarding the distribution of exercises for all the hours of the day; for thus they will be always occupied.

To avoid all disunion the Superior shall studiously train up the Novices in the perfect spirit of charity, and cause them to observe all that has been said in the Second Part of these Constitutions. There, the practice of charity is insinuated towards all, but particularly towards the Sisters; and the necessary

---

* Gal. 6.

corrections laid down for the slightest **violation** of union and charity.

If, in any house, there be characters altogether irreconcilable with the rest of the Community, they shall be separated and changed to other houses, with the permission of the Bishop, or of the Spiritual Father.

The Sisters should remember that their Community is a body of which Jesus Christ is the Head; that they should bear with and sympathize with each other; as the members of the same body assist one another. If at variance among themselves, they would cause more bitter grief to their adorable Head than by rending His arm or hand, because the spiritual union of charity between the members of His mystic body is stronger and more close than the material union between the members of His natural body.

Should it happen, either through violence of temper, or misunderstanding, that any quarrel take place between Sisters, we order them to be immediately reconciled; and, on no account, shall they retire to rest without a renewal of friendship. We also forbid them to speak of their disunions among themselves, and, much less, to persons unconnected with the Congregation, even though they were their relatives or their dearest friends; for their Sisters and the Congregation should be more dear to them than the whole world. **Neither** should the faults of Sisters **be a** cause of bad example to seculars, and of contempt for the Congregation. The Superior shall severely, and without exception, punish any infraction of this regulation.

CHAPTER X.

OF THE MEANS OF AVOIDING TOO MUCH INTERCOURSE WITH LAY PERSONS.

As there is nothing that so well preserves us in union with God as the flight of the world and the love of retirement, so there is nothing that so much dissipates the soul and separates it from God as communication with the world. If, then, our Sisters sincerely desire to preserve themselves in union with God, to which they are bound by their holy profession, they must love holy retirement, and fly, as much as possible, all commerce with persons of the world; and never go among them, unless when obedience, necessity or charity oblige them to it. This is the most powerful reason for their avoiding the visits of seculars.

For these reasons, we order all Superiors of houses to cause the following rules to be observed :

1. They shall never allow Sisters to receive the visits of any men, whether lay or ecclesiastical, without giving them a companion who shall be present during the entire visit; and said companion is bound in con-

science to inform the Superior if, on occasion of such visits, anything be observed in the slightest degree blameable.

2. The visits of relatives are to be permitted, if not too frequent; in which case the Superiors will excuse the Sisters from appearing, because contrary to the regulations of the Congregation. If Sisters admit of such visits without permission of the Superior, or maintain a written or other correspondence with seculars, without due permission, the Superior shall correct them; and if the correction be not effectual, such Sisters shall be removed to another house. Should this remedy not correct the evil, such Sisters shall be dismissed from the Congregation.

3. They shall also prevent the visits from being long, and in no case should they suffer them to exceed half an hour.

4. They should most especially take care, that when Sisters go out to visit the sick, or for any other business, they shall not, under any pretext whatever, make any visit without their express permission. Sisters violating this rule are to be kept at home, and have such other penance imposed on them as the Superiors shall judge proper.

5. They shall avoid receiving the frequent visits of females, and Sisters shall always have a companion present during such visits.

CHAPTER XI.

OF AVOIDING MANY DIRECTORS.

As the body has but one head to guide it, so the soul should have but one Director, according to the reflection of spiritual writers. The Sisters, then, shall have but one Director.—Whenever a new Director is to be appointed, they should offer up their most fervent prayers to God, that he would vouchsafe to send them one according to His Divine Will.

When the Spiritual Guide shall be appointed, all the Sisters will receive him with great confidence; and the Superior shall not, except on every extraordinary occasions, allow any other to be sent for; which, besides, can be done only with the approbation of the Bishop. The desire of changing confessors is owing either to weakness of character, or attachment to one's own will; and Superiors shall endeavor to convince the Sisters that it is contrary to the Constitutions, and that they have all the necessary means of their sanctification in the actual state of things.

CHAPTER XII.

OF THE MEANS OF AVOIDING RESTRAINT IN MATTERS OF CONSCIENCE.

Though all the Sisters go to the same confessor, yet, to avoid the inconveniences which restraint in matters of conscience might at times occasion, and to satisfy the weakness of certain souls, we allow the Sisters to write to the Bishop or to the Spiritual Father whenever they please; as also to apply for an Extraordinary Confessor, when required. But that this permission may not give rise to any inconvenience, the Superior shall observe the following regulations:

1. She shall see that when an Extraordinary Confessor is required, he be approved of by the Bishop, and authorized by him to hear the confessions of religious.

2. She shall not send for the Extraordinary Confessor except once in three months; and should any Sisters demand him more frequently, the Superior may grant it or not, as she may judge expedient; remembering it is right to afford perfect liberty of conscience, but that it would be very wrong to encourage an excessive desire of change, a foolish curiosity, vanity, or pride.

3. The Extraordinary Confessor shall be consulted only in the confessional, with the usual precautions required by the Church in hearing confessions.

4. Although it is not advisable to send for the Extraordinary Confessor too frequently, it is a good practice in well regulated religious orders, to require that all the religious go to confession once or twice a year to the Extraordinary Confessor.

CHAPTER XIII.

OF THE OBLIGATIONS OF THE SISTERS OF KNOWING AND KEEPING THEIR CONSTITUTIONS.

When the Lord gave his commandments and laws to His people, He said to them: "Lay up these My words in your hearts, and in your minds, and hang them for a sign on your hands, and place them between your eyes, meditate on them when thou sittest in thy house, and when thou walkest on the way, and when thou liest down and risest up. Thou shalt write them on the posts and the doors of thy house. Behold I set forth in your sight this day a blessing and a curse. A blessing, if you obey the commandments of the Lord your God; a curse if you obey not the commandments of the Lord your God."*

Having laid down in these Constitutions all the rules necessary for the salvation and perfection of the Sisters of our Congregation, we exhort them, in the person of Almighty God, who has called them, and to whom they have made a vow of obedience and fidelity, to study well these Constitutions, which God has given them, through their Superiors; to love them, to meditate on them, to practise them with an inviolable exactness, in order thus to secure their immortal souls, and to contribute as far as they are able to the preser-

---
* Deuteron. 11.

vation of their Congregation in that state of perfection of which they make profession. Finally, we exhort them to reflect on the blessing which God promises to those who obey His laws, and to beware of the curse with which He threatens those souls who are ignorant of, or who despise and trangress His laws.

That the Sisters may know all their rules, and that there be no excuse for ignorance regarding them, we order all Superiors to keep several copies of these Constitutions, and to provide every person belonging to their Community with a copy. We desire that every one, without exception, read, every day, a Chapter of the Constitutions, or some one of the maxims of virtue, or some practice in the Directory. We ordain, that the Superiors cause a chapter of it to be read one day of each week, namely, on Friday, and that they frequently explain parts of it, in the Chapter to be held for the avowal of faults.

That our Sisters be not troubled with scruples of conscience, or fears of having committed mortal sin, in violating the rules, we declare that our Constitutions do not, of themselves, oblige under mortal sin, no more than those of other religious orders, unless in the following circumstances, explained by St. Francis de Sales.

1. When the thing forbidden by these Constitutions is, in itself, a mortal sin, and

the thing commanded be necessary to salvation.

2. When a person acts, or when a person refuses to comply with the rule through pure contempt of the Constitutions.

3. When a person refuses obedience to the Superior, imposed in these or similar words: "I command you to obey, under pain of mortal sin." But the Superior should not make use of such forms of commanding, except in cases of the greatest importance, and with the concurrence of the Bishop or of the Spiritual Father.

4. When the Bishop commands or forbids anything under pain of excommunication.

5. When one would transgress a rule contrary to the essential vows of poverty, chastity or obedience, and other important matters concerning the Constitutions, or contrary to the religious life. If, for example, a person were to take, or keep, or give away anything considerable without permission; or if a person were to resist, through contempt, the orders of the Superiors; or if a Sister were to consent to thoughts, or say words, or act contrary to chastity; also, by leaving the Congregation without dispensation; and such like matters.

6. When the violation of a rule gives scandal, the consequences of which inflict great injury on the Congregation, or on any one of its houses.

7. When a fault is committed against the rules through any excessive passion: for example, to omit exercises of piety, as the Office, Prayer, Confession, Communion, through sloth; to eat out of meals through gluttony; to violate silence through anger. From the examples adduced, it appears that though faults may not be mortal in virtue of the rules, they become mortal in consequence of circumstances which would render them mortal even in a lay person: as to transgress a law through contempt; to eat a small portion through great gluttony; to violate a vow; to scandalize one's neighbor; to pursue anything though excessive passion.

The Constitutions, then, of themselves, do not oblige under sin; but it is extremely difficult to violate rules without the act being sinful from circumstances independent of the rule.

And the Sisters should, therefore, fear the violation of them, according to the words of the Wise Man: "He that feareth God, neglecteth nothing."* Again, the Sisters should remember that their vocation is a special grace, of which they must render an account at the moment of death. And they should keep impressed on their minds the other words of the Wise Man: "He that neglecteth his own way shall die."† Now the

---

* Eccle. 7. † Prov. 19.

way of the Sisters are their Constitutions, by the exact observance of which, they should advance from virtue to virtue, till they behold their Eternal Spouse in Holy Sion. If they should neglect this way, or depart from its exact observance, they would lose the way of life; they would walk in that of death; and, consequently, they should adhere to it all the days of their life with all prudence, with vigilance and solicitude; like the wise virgins, always ready for the coming of their Spouse, Jesus Christ. The fate of the five foolish virgins should make the Sisters fear to loiter in the way, either to the right or to the left, but cause them to go on in the straight way that leads to life, by means of which they will experience the effect of these words of St. Paul: "Whoever shall follow this rule, peace on them and mercy."*

MAXIMS OF PERFECTION.

We exhort all our Sisters to observe with exactness the following maxims, which contain the spirit of their Institute and Constitutions:

1. Have always before your eyes the end of your vocation, which is most sublime; and never do anything unworthy of one who makes profession of modesty, meekness and sanctity.

---
* Gal. 6.

2. Let it be the general rule of your life to be perfect, as your Father in Heaven is perfect; that is, to embrace in all things what tends to the greater glory of God, what is most conformable to His Divine Will, and what is most agreeable in His eyes.

3. Humble yourself, in honor of the Incarnate Word, who humbled Himself with such love for your sake; and practise the most sincere and profound humility towards all and on all occasions; but most particularly towards God, who alone can bless the Institute.

4. Lead a life of the most pure and perfect charity, in honor of your Divine Spouse, the Holy Ghost.

5. Make no more account of the world, and of its vanities than of smoke; that is, despise this world of shadows, and dread its maxims, which are full of malice and impiety.

6. Put off entirely the old man, and put on the new.

7. Lead a life altogether dead to the world, to self-love and to self-will; be mild, humble of heart; be simple, modest; maintain an interior and exterior peace; be replete with charity towards all:—in a word, let your life be modelled after that of Jesus Christ, whom you should copy in all things. Thus you may hope to draw multitudes to God by your example and conversation.

8. In respect to zeal, the **distinctive mark**

of our profession, imitate those who are most zealous; embrace in desire the salvation and perfection of the whole world, with a generous zeal and courage which would incline you to do all, to suffer and undertake all for the advancement of God's glory, and the salvation of your dear fellow-creatures.

9. Place the strength of your resolutions and the hopes of your enterprises on the knowledge of weakness, the total distrust of yourselves, and the firm and assured confidence you have in God, to whom nothing is hard or impossible, and who will most certainly assist you in all that you undertake for His glory under the influence of grace and in obedience to orders.

10. Fly, incessantly, and with extreme horror, all vanity, complacency, and infidelity to God's grace, as pests which infect good works and which turn off the course of the Divine benedictions from our lives and actions.

11. Never speak well or ill of yourselves, without some unavoidable necessity. Never think well of yourselves, neither for what you may do, because all what you are and can do, is nothing before God; and because, in every respect, you are replete with such imperfections as would render you objects of infinite contempt to yourself, if they were known to you.

12. Speak well always of others; esteem highly the good they do; and excuse and con-

ceal as much as you can, the wrong they may do.

13. Prefer to suffer all the evils of time than the least which may affect eternity; all the evils of nature, than the least of grace; for every motive persuades us that we should adopt this maxim.

14. In order more clearly to explain the above-mentioned maxim, embrace rather the loss of all goods, and endure all evils, than to sin, however slightly, against the most holy will of God.

15. Be humble, since whatever you are, whatever you have, and whatever you do for yourself or others, proceeds from a pure act of God's mercy, of which, as also of the assistance of His grace, you render yourself unworthy if you are not humble in all things.

16. Be also most faithful to the grace of the Holy Ghost, listening attentively to His inspirations; obeying Him promptly and entirely; and giving glory to Him, as is just, for the success of all your good actions.

17. Have God, in all things, and everywhere, before your eyes: esteem only His will, His glory, and make no account of anything else.

18. Desire little in this world; be not over-eager for what you may desire—that is, live without desire; resign yourself, most perfectly, to the loving Providence of God, your Father.

19. Make so perfect a sacrifice of yourself and of will, that you may no longer live to yourself, that you no longer deliberatly desire anything, unless that the will of God be entirely accomplished in you and in all others.

20. Acknowledge and tenderly cherish this most amiable will of God, in all the accidents of life, whatever they may be; and in all the orders of your Superiors, unless any thing manifestly sinful be commanded.

21. Apply yourself seriously and entirely to do, at the present moment, and with perfection, the will of God, without occupying your mind unnecessarily with what God or your Superiors may exact of you at any future period.

22. Seek no praise or recompense for your good works in this life, that you may receive greater and more enduring reward in eternity.

23. Let your good actions be hidden in time, and known only to God, that they may appear in eternity, or never appear, if such be the will of God.

24. Love nothing but God, and what is divine; belong entirely to God by a holy abandonment of yourself; act entirely for God by a pure love and total disinterestedness; remain entirely in God by a continual remembrance and study of His presence; live entirely according to God, by the con-

formity of your will, your life, and all things to Him.

25. Rejoice in all things for the sole glory of God, by whomsoever it is promoted; and rejoice more that His glory is promoted by others than by yourself.

26. Seek in all things that God may be satisfied with you, and nothing more. The better to practise this maxim, remember during life, in afflictions, sickness, and other trials, to desire solely that which renders God more pleased, without regard to your own interests.

27. Love the interior life of Jesus Christ, as far as is compatible with the duties of charity and zeal.

28. Regret that the world thinks of you, if any one entertains affection for you. Believe this truth, that its thoughts and affections are uselessly bestowed on persons who so little merit them. Desire only that the thoughts and affections of men and angels be fixed on God solely, or that they be solely for God. Believe with Teresa, the truths of religion, with a more firm faith by how much the more incomprehensible they are.

29. And for similar reasons, in the practice of hope, confide the more in God, when, according to your views, there is less appearance of human aid or success, and when great difficulties oppose your enterprises.

30. In your greatest troubles and dangers hope with unshaken confidence, not that God will always comfort you, but that he will effect in you, and through you, His most holy and amiable will; and live perfectly content with this expectation.

31. When you appear to be abandoned by God and all creatures, call to mind the abandonment of Jesus in the Garden and on the Cross, and willingly embrace your own trials, in consideration of His.

32. Seek to please God in such a manner, by each one of your actions, as if you alone ought to labor for His glory, and no one practised the same actions.

33. In all your enterprises, take care that God be the principle and end of them; in their progress, depart not from His holy will; and as to their success be perfectly satisfied, whether the desired object be obtained or not. Wish, in all things and everywhere, that God's will be accomplished; which Divine Will you should equally love and recognize in the delay and frustration of your laudable designs, as in their advancement and happy success.

34. Be persuaded, that in all places and and in all your actions, God sees and examines you: do not, then, in his presence what you would not presume to do before any one whom you respected.

35. Love and act according to reason and

duty, and not from caprice and natural inclination.

36. Ask for nothing but what pleases God; refuse nothing that pleases God, maintaining a perfect resignation to His Divine will.

37. As to the fulfilment of your request, or regarding your refusals, complain not of others, but alone of yourself.

38. Live not of yourself, but entirely for God and your neighbor; esteem nothing but what is eternal.

39. Let your first and universal intention be, to resemble your Saviour in all things; cause Him to be abide in you, and do you abide in Him.

40. Sigh, alone and incessantly, after the love of God, and of your Divine Jesus, but without anxiety or uneasiness.

41. Be, at least in desire, the poorest in the world, the most humble and the most humbled, the most pure and obedient, in order to be like Him, who was the most poor and humble, and who is the Divine example according to whom you should form yourself.

42. Be always serious in your intercourse with strangers, but at the same time respectful.

43. Live with your Saviour attached to the cross; die to pleasures; embrace ignominy; live alone for God, and die entirely to yourself.

44. If there be many things to be done at

the same time in the Community, and the choice is left to you, do you choose what is most humbling and difficult, and leave to others what is easiest and most honorable.

45. Seek in all things the glory of God, your own salvation and perfection, and that of your neighbor, and not the sweets and consolations which are frequently met with in the Divine service.

46. Be most condescending **towards** your neighbor, particularly to**wards the** untoward and refractory; and, **however difficult** it may be, let not, if possible, **your repugnance** appear; but always preserve **a cheerful countenance**, full of sweetness, as if you derived pleasure from what was to you most painful. In all that you do for your neighbor, endeavor to be actuated by the same sentiments of devotion and charity as if you were attending on the person of Jesus Christ.

47. Always prefer the good will and pleasure of your neighbor to your own, provided God be not offended nor less honored.

48. Bestow cordially all the favors you can on those towards whom you feel the greatest repugnance. This was the practice of Saint Aloysius de Gonzaga.

49. Interpret everything in the most favorable sense.

50. Let your heart be always free and unattached to anything earthly, however **good and virtuous the appearances may be.**

51. Destroy all human respect and vicious condescension, and make, with a generous heart, a resolution never to do anything however small, that is displeasing to God.

52. When you labor for your neighbor, be quite disinterested; look for no recompense. Let the happiness of assisting others and of pleasing God be your sole desire.

53. When what you do pleases others, tremble, instead of taking complacency at it; for Saint Paul says, those who please men are not the servants of Jesus Christ.

54. After performing any good work, give all the glory of it to Christ, who, by His death, has truly become the Principle of our life and of our good actions.

55. Be persuaded of this truth, that you scarcely do anything but put obstacles in the way of Divine Grace.

56. However successful may be your good works, be persuaded that the sins you have committed during your life will be the cause of much less progress than what Almighty God might have expected from your co-operation.

57. Cherish alone interior sweetness of soul, living in peace and in the calm subjection of all your passions. In regard to your exterior, do all things without precipitation, bearing all the untoward occurrences of life without complaint, murmur, or disquietude.

58. Have tender and strong affections for

the tranquil and intimate union with God; for the most cordial charity and forbearance towards your neighbor; for perfect purity of heart; for true charity and fidelity to grace, accompanied with a sweet death to nature; lowly humility; with the most ingenuous simplicity and sincere candor; with obedience which requires no reasonings; with the most abject poverty; with continual joy of mind, suitable to your Institute; in a word, have the pure and perfect love of God, which may animate all things in you.

59. Be satisfied with the ordinary course of virtue and life which you have chosen.

60. Consider the accidents which happen to you as most useful, and not as obstacles; cherish them as the effects of a most loving Providence towards you.

61. Study to exhibit kindness to all, and unkindness to none.

62. Be exact and diligent in the discharge of those things which are recommended to you, or which are duties of your office, especially where the utility or necessity of your neighbor is concerned. Take care of the fault of those who omit such duties, for these things which are more in accordance with humor or interest.

63. Be courageous in undertaking what God desires of you, and constant in executing it; never relinquishing it, whatever difficulties may arise, unless you be

placed in an utter incapability of accomplishing your purpose.

64. According to the same maxim, pursue to the end, with sweetness and firmness, what you have once resolved on, and what you reasonably believe is for the greater glory of God.

65. Look with suspicion on all undertakings and desires which are begun with uneasiness and ardor, and which distract you from your important and necessary duties.

66. Never think on the future, except in connection with the present, but refer all to the Providence of God.

67. Do not inquire what your Superiors may purpose regarding you, but leave all in the hands of God.

68. Be content with the employment which obedience has assigned to you, applying yourself to it with diligence, without the slightest thought of change, until obedience may appoint otherwise.

69. Be always ready to obey, and indifferent to all that is not contrary to the law of God; to live or die, to be in health or in sickness, placing your entire happiness in the sole accomplishment of the will of God.

70. Have one only desire, namely—to be such as God desires you to be, in nature, grace and glory, for time and eternity.

71. Obey promptly, cheerfully and simply, without allowing a single thought of repug-

nance or refusal to intervene between the command and the execution, unless it be sinful.

72. Desire that others think little of you and much of every one else: be grieved that you should be esteemed, but happy that others be esteemed.

73. Hide, in the best way you can, the little grace which God may confer on you; and, when you can do so with discretion, make known what may render you despicable.

74. Fulfil the duties of great and sincere love, and you will be perfect.

75. Glory in contempt, and receive confusion, not only with patience, but with joy and thanks. In confusion and scorn courageous souls find treasures of grace, merit, and celestial benedictions.

76. Be happy that others possess more genius and talent than yourself, more grace, and even more virtue; and let it be your delight that God's Divine Will is accomplished in that respect.

77. Hold it as an undoubted maxim, that one is not more holy when one commits less faults, and practises virtue more easily; but one is more indebted to God's grace, which often renders those who begin a spiritual life more fervent in good works, and less subject to fault than persons who are more advanced. Sanctity consists in a hidden gift, known alone to God.

78. Whatever virtue you may be thought to possess, does not dispense you from a sincere and humble fear of the Lord, knowing that the judgments of God are inscrutable and that His sentiments are different from those of men.

79. Be persuaded, that in the exercise of your zeal, there is nothing so excellent as the disinterested and strong yearnings of the soul after God's glory, which he condescends to communicate to creatures utterly unworthy of them.

80. However pure your intentions and views may appear, be still persuaded that you seek yourself in some recess of your heart.

81. Do not anticipate grace by any indiscreet precipitation, but quietly wait its movements; and when it comes, follow it with great humility, sweetness, fidelity and courage.

82. Advance good works till near their completion; and then, if it can be done unobservedly, let others perfect them and gain all the credit.

83. Though you are nothing of yourself, be superior to everything that is not God; not suffering yourself to be influenced by creatures, but keeping them all subject to reason and virtue.

84. Despise all the appearances of virtue which you think you perceive in yourself, looking on them as deceitful images; re-

membering, that from yourself you have only sin and imperfection, and that Christ tells the servants who have done all that is commanded, to say "*We are unprofitable servants.*" *

85. Treasure up carefully time, which is of infinite value. Lose not a minute of it, but offering it up, and consecreating it to God without waste.

86. Profit by the occasions which present themselves of practising virtues in a sublime degree.

87. Perform with great diligence and perfection your ordinary actions, and guard against remissness.

88. Be of noble mind; which will make you regard all that is not God as nothing; and embrace sweetly and ardently every enterprise of zeal, suggested by the Holy Ghost.

89. Whatever you may do or suffer, look on it as nothing, as it indeed is, if compared with the greatness of God and His infinite perfections.

90. Do not imagine you are arrived to the true love of God, unless this sacred love has annihilated in you all kind of vanity, pusillanimity, coldness, tepidity, sensuality, earthly affection and attachment,—in a word, all that is corrupt in your nature, making you live

---

* Luke 17.

by the movements of grace, and according to the maxims of Jesus Christ.

91. Desire the perfection suitable to the three powers of your soul; for the memory a general forgetfulness of all things, and even of self, that you may remember God alone; for the understanding, to see God in all things, His glory, His power, His providence, His mercy; for the will, the liberty of approaching God, of loving Him, and of embracing all the orders of His Providence with all the affection of your soul.

92. Watch over yourself, and take care not to allow yourself to be deceived by the demon, under the appearance of an angel of light, who often proposes the suggestions of nature for the movements of grace, and fanciful instincts and rash delusions for real inspirations and revelations of God.

93. Study to arrive at the state of perfect indifference, of entire resignation to God's will, of holy abandonment of yourself to His gracious Providence, of loving acquiescence in His pleasure in all the accidents and occurrences of life, of tender affection for the most pure will of God, of ardent desire of being according to His heart,—in other words, aspire to a perfect conformity of your will to the Divine Will.

94. When you enjoy the presence of Divine grace, and the inestimable sweets of the love of God, bear in mind that this

treasure does not belong to you; it is only lent or given you; that you are indebted for it to your Saviour Jesus Christ, who can take it from you when he pleases, without any injustice; and if He withdraw His graces from you, all the good you appear to possess vanishes like smoke.

95. Be fortified against human fears in encountering difficulties and contradictions, hoping then more than ever in the Divine aid, when all things would seem to impel you to despair.

96. Do not sigh to be released from life, when overwhelmed by crosses: it is sufficient for you to be crucified in Jesus Christ, as much and in the way it may please God; leave to Him the disposition of all the moments of your life and of your death.

97. Union and communication with God is indispensable, in order to practise the above maxims, and all virtues, because a continual influence of His graces and our own co-operation produce virtuous acts in our souls. God communicates these graces in greater or less degree, according as His creatures are more or less united with Him. Labor, then, without ceasing, to maintain this union with your God.

98. The virtues which will enable you to acquire and maintain this most desirable union, and which form, as it were, the compendium of our Institute, are—

Great purity of heart and of intention;
A profound humility in all things;
A perfect mortification of self-love, one's own judgment, of the will, of the senses, which should extend to the annihilation of the inclinations;
A most faithful obedience to all the movements of grace;
An ingenuous simplicity, accompanied with prudence;
An entire detachment from creatures, a renunciation of self;
A peace and sweetness which suffers and acts without disquietude or hurry;
An entire abandonment of one's self into the hands of Providence, with an absolute dependence upon God;
The love of retirement and prayer;
Perfect charity for all, which loves all without exception—purely, perseveringly, and equally in God and for God.
Finally, a pure love of God, which makes the soul think constantly of God, with whom it seeks unceasingly a closer union, after whom it ever languishes.

99. Ah! Jesus, mercifully distribute the forenamed virtues to all those called to this Institute, and do not allow, on any account, that any be admitted who are not desirous of acquiring them.

DIRECTORY
FOR
THE SISTERS OF ST. JOSEPH.

We have complied this small Directory, in order that our sisters learn by it to practise devoutly all the exercises of piety which are commanded in the Fifth part of the Constitutions, for every day, week, month and year. It is divided into four parts. In the first, we shall treat of the exercises of every day, in the second, of those every week, in the third, of those every month; and in the fourth of the annual exercises.

PART I.

Of the Exercises of Every Day.

CHAPTER I.

OF RISING IN THE MORNING.

On awaking in the morning, be careful to **give** your first thoughts to God, saying with all your heart, and even with the mouth, for greator fervor, these, or such like words:—"I adore Thee, O my God; I thank Thee; I give myself entirely to Thee. My Lord Jesus, when shall I be Thine entirely and perfectly, according to Thy heart? My God and my All, I love Thee with my whole heart, in Thee are all my hopes." After that turn your thoughts on the points of the morning's meditation.

If it should happen that you were to awake any time before the hour of rising, make some pious reflections; consider yourself as buried in the immensity of the Divine Essence as in an ocean of bounty, of love, and light; imagine your Saviour present, as also the Glorious Virgin, Saint Joseph (your Patron), and your Angel Guardian, thank them for the care they have taken of you during the night. Reflect how many poor persons there are badly clad, exposed to the inclemency of the weather. Excite such and similar affections in your heart.

If you have any difficult business on hand recommend it to God, to Mary, to your Angel Guardian. Also, if you have any trial or affliction, ask for light and consolation.

In rising, commence by making the sign of the Cross: afterwards pronounce devoutly the sweet names of *Jesus*, *Maria*, and *Joseph*.

Take your clothes and, with modesty dressing yourself, say—" Blessed be the Holy and Undivided Trinity, now and for evermore. Amen. Blessed be God the Father, who created me to His image; blessed be God the Son, who redeemed me by His most precious blood; and God the Holy Ghost, who called me to a religious state, and who conferred so many graces on me whilst I am in it, which, unhappily, I have greatly abused. Blessed be the Glorious Virgin. St. Joseph, my Patron, my Angel Guardian, and all the Angels and Saints of Heaven. Recite the *Pater, Ave,* and *Credo.*

In dressing, occupy your mind with some holy thoughts, as, for example, the consideration of what ornaments your poor soul may have; what virtues; is it clothed with Divine graces; and try, according to the advice of St. Paul, to put on Jesus Christ, by the imitation of His Life, Passion and Death. When dressed, kneel down, and adore profoundly your God; kiss the ground, with the thought that before the Divine Majesty you are nothing but dust and ashes, and that after your death you shall return to dust.

You might also kiss the ground with devotion, as Jesus and Mary trod upon it. O how sweet is this practice to devout souls!

Go afterwards to the chapel to adore your Lord; but if that be not in your power, make your offering before the altar in your oratory in the following manner:—

"My God, my Creator, and my All, prostrate before Thy Sovereign Majesty I adore Thee with profound respect; I believe in Thee; I hope in Thee; I love Thee with my whole heart; I render Thee infinite thanks for all Thy benefits, especially for having preserved me during the past night from so many evils. I humbly ask pardon for all my sins, I detest them purely for Thy love, and because they displease Thee. In fine, I offer to Thee, in union with the Life, Passion, and Death of my Saviour, all that I shall think, say and perform during this day, and, also, whatever I shall suffer, I wish to bear it with resignation and patience, as coming from Thy hands. Give me Thy bendictions; take me under Thy protection; grant me the grace of passing this day, and all the days of my life, without offending Thee. Glorious Virgin Mary, holy Patriarch St. Joseph, Angels and Saints of Heaven, and especially thou, my good Angel, take me under thy protection, and give me thy benediction. Amen.

CHAPTER II.

OF THE MEDITATION.

The Sisters shall follow the method of meditation prescribed by St. Francis de Sales, in the second part of the Introduction to a Devout Life. They shall read and learn the rules which he gives for practising with facility and effect this holy exercise, which is one of the most essential for their sanctification. We shall give here an abridgment of it, of which they can ordinarily make use.

To be enabled to enter on this first and most important duty of prayer by meditation, the Sisters should aspire to great union with God, live in His presence, mortify their passions, restrain their senses, be ever ready to receive His visits, and keep themselves near Him. Otherwise, they will experience a thousand difficulties, and they will lose much time, when they would wish to collect themselves for their meditation. Spiritual writers call this presence of God, the remote preparation for meditation.

This prayer has three parts, namely—preparation, meditation and conclusion.

In the preparation, there are three acts to be made. First, to place one's self in the presence of God; secondly, to invoke His aid and lights; thirdly, to propose the subject of meditation. In the meditation there are three things to be done: the first is—to consider and deeply to penetrate the truths proposed; secondly, to move the heart to pious affections; thirdly, make strong resolutions to practise the good, or to correct the evil or fault which has been the subject of the meditation, or to which the meditation actually refers.

The conclusion has, also, three acts; the first is, to thank God for the graces bestowed on us during the prayer; the second, to offer to Him the affections and good resolutions formed; thirdly, to ask the grace of practising faithfully the affections and good resolutions made during the prayer.

In order to put in practice this method, you will kneel down, mortify your senses, keep a particular watch over your eyes, let your mind be collected within itself, banish every thought except God and the subject of your meditations, and God, who makes His vioce heard in solitude, will communicate Himself to you. When you are thus recollected, you should begin your prayer by the preparation.

First—You shall make an act of faith, persuading yourself firmly and in a lively manner of God's presence, that you are immersed in His Divine Essence.

Secondly—Acknowledge yourself unworthy to appear before the Divine Majesty, on account of your miseries and sins; that you are unable to form a good thought; beg pardon, then, for all your sins, and ask all those lights and graces you require to perform your meditation well.

Thirdly—Propose to your mind the subject which you should have previously read; and if you do not remember the points, you can read them again. It is of the greatest importance to read the points of the meditation the evening previous.

You will now proceed to the second part of your prayer, in which:

First—You will apply your mind to consider well, and examine all the circumstances of the subject you may have chosen, and you shall reason on them till you have penetrated them thoroughly.

Secondly—After these considerations, stir up in your heart pious emotions and holy affections, which may lead your will to the love and practice of what is good, or hatred and disgust of the evil on which you have meditated.

Thirdly—Form strong resolutions to follow the holy sentiments with which God has favored you, by proposing in particular to put them in practice on such and such occasions.

You shall now proceed to the third part of your prayer, which is the conclusion, in which:

First—Return thanks to God for all the lights, affections, and resolutions which you have received from His Divine bounty.

Secondly—Offer them all in union with the merits of His Divine Son, Jesus Christ, acknowledging that it is through His goodness and the sole merit of His Divine Son, that these favors have been granted to you.

Thirdly—Ask Him for the grace of fulfilling faithfully all the good resolutions and affections, remembering that as His Divine grace was required to form them in your heart, so it is equally necessary to preserve them and to reduce them to practice.

Having made this conclusion, ask pardon of the Almighty for all the distractions and negligences committed in the course of the prayer.

Select then two or three of the most holy and touching thoughts or resolutions with which God favored you, and which may appear most adapted to your spiritual wants, to serve as a spiritual nosegay, which by its fragrance will refresh your soul during the whole day.

You shall not devote more than about half a quarter of an hour to the three acts of the preparation, and about the same time in the three acts of the conclusion; and all the remainder of the time you shall employ in the three acts of considerations, affections and resolutions, which are the most important and most profitable occupations of all prayer.

You should endeavor, after your prayer or meditation, to preserve in your heart the good sentiments with which God may have favored you; and take care not to become so entirely distracted and dissipated exteriorly, as not to be interiorly in communication with God, practising the good resolutions with which He inspired you, and which you promised in your morning meditation. Endeavor, then, from time to time, during the day, to recall to mind the affections you conceived and the resolutions you made. This is the work of time, to be obtained by persevering prayer. Again, it may be said that the perfect spirit of prayer is the greatest of all God's graces; for it brings every other grace with it; it obtains all things for us, as Christ assures us; we should, therefore, never desist from our efforts in studying to become true religious in the practice of sublime prayer.

CHAPTER III.

OF THE OFFICE, AND OF VOCAL PRAYER.

You should entertain the greatest respect and esteem for Vocal Prayer, and the Office; since Jesus Christ often prayed, and taught us to pray vocally, especially when he taught his disciples the *Pater Noster*. He also sang the praises of His Father; the Angels and Saints of heaven eternally sing them. The Holy Spirit, who governs the Church on earth, teaches the faithful to sing the Divine praises perpetually in the Divine Offices.

When, therefore, you assist at the Office, or at Vocal Prayer, be present with great respect, bearing in mind that you are about to join with the celestial choirs of Angels and Saints, and even with Jesus Himself, and also all the Church of Christ on earth, in singing the praises of your God. Beware, then, not to go at random, with precipitation to prayer, but leave all strange thoughts at the door, and appear before God in great recollection when you pray.

Before you begin your prayer, place yourself in the Divine Presence; ask, with great humility and confidence, the grace of praying well. Invoke the Holy Ghost, if you can, by saying, *Veni Creator.* Place yourself in the Heart of Jesus; unite your prayers with His, your intention and attention in prayer with His, with those of the Angels, of the Saints, and the whole Church in Heaven and on earth. Pray and sing with them, thinking on the Infinite Majesty of God, whom you address, and who condescends to listen to you, though the sublimest spirits of Heaven tremble at the sight of His greatness.

During prayer, observe the greatest exterior and interior modesty, not allowing, as far as may be possible, any distraction of the mind, or unnecessary stirring of the body, or any unbecoming posture.

Be attentive to pronounce the words distinctly and slowly, to follow the meaning of the words; and if you say the Divine Office, which you may not understand, fix your thoughts on God, who hears with pleasure what you say, because His Divine Spirit inspired every word of the Psalms and Canticles pronounced by you.

When you pronounce the words, *Gloria Patri, et Filio,* and the names of Jesus, of Mary and Joseph, bow the head in reverence, making a lower inclination at the words *Gloria Patri* and of *Jesus.*

Remember, according to what we read in the lives of the Saints, that the Angels write the words of our prayers in gold or silver, or ink or water, according to the devotion and attention we have in reciting our prayers.

After the Office and other prayers, return thanks to God for allowing you to sing His praises, and pray to His Divine Majesty, and ask pardon for the faults you have committed during them.

CHAPTER IV.

ON THE MASS.

As Mass is the greatest act of religion, you ought to assist at it with extraordinary devotion, attention and reverence, which is done by following this method:—

When you hear the sound of the bell calling you to Mass, remember that as the people of Jerusalem were invited by the sound of trumpets to witness the Crucifixion of Jesus Christ, so also by the sound of this bell you are called to assist at the tremendous Sacrifice of the Mass, in which His Passion and Death are renewed, by offering up on the altar the same Body and Blood which were immolated on Calvary.

On the way to the church, represent to yourself the holy women who followed Jesus, carrying his Cross to Calvary, where they beheld Him expire, and go, with a piety similar to theirs, to see Him sacrificed and die anew on the altar. Having entered the church, take holy water, and beg of God, that, in virtue of it, you may be purified, be made worthy to appear before Him, and that it may preserve you from the temptations of the demon. Then kneel down, adore most profoundly the most adorable Sacrament of the altar, and say the following acts previously to Mass:—

Act of Faith.

O my God, I most firmly believe that the holy Mass is a true sacrifice, in which the priest offers to Thee the same Body and the same Blood of Thy Son Jesus Christ, who was crucified on the Cross.

Act of Contrition.

My God, I ask pardon, with all my heart, for all my sins; I am extremely sorry for having committed them, because they are displeasing to Thee. I would rather die than commit them again. Pardon me, I beseech Thee; and give me thy grace, that I may devoutly assist at this adorable Sacrifice.

Direct your Intention.

My God, I unite my prayers and intentions with those of Thy Divine Son Jesus Christ, with those of the priest, and of the whole Church; with them I offer Thee the Holy Sacrifice of the Mass—

First—to render Thee infinite honor and glory, and to repair the multiplied injuries we have offered to thy Divine Majesty.

Secondly—I offer it in thanksgiving for the infinite favors received of Thy Divine bounty;

Thirdly—I offer it to appease Thy wrath, to satisfy Thy justice, and to obtain the pardon of my sins;

Fourthly—I offer it, also, that, through the merits of Jesus Christ, Thou mayest grant us all those graces and virtues we require in order to please Thee and serve Thee till death, and that thou mayest grant to the souls in Purgatory the deliverance from their pains, or the diminution of them.

Fifthly—I offer it in memory of the **Death** and Passion of Thy Son Jesus Christ.

Prayer.

"My God, I beseech Thee, through the intercession of the most Blessed Virgin and of all the Saints, and through the assistance of my good Angel, to preserve me from all temptations, irreverences and distractions, and to grant me, during the Holy Sacrifice, a continual attention to Thy Divine Majesty, and a great devotion to the Passion and Death of Thy Son Jesus Christ. Amen."

When you have said these acts and prayers, in preparation for the Sacrifice, you will meditate, from the commencement of the Mass to the end, on the mysteries of the Life, Passion and Death of Jesus Christ, which are strikingly represented in it. Meditate on His Incarnation, by which He loaded Himself with our sins, from the beginning to the end of the Confiteor, or " *I confess ;*" on the Nativity, at the " *Glory be to God on high;*" on His hidden life, to the age of thirty, at the prayers before the epistle: meditate on His preaching, during the *Epistle* and *Gospel*; on the designs of the Jews to waylay and put Him to death at the *Offertory ;* on His triumphant entry into Jerusalem, at the *Preface ;* on His capture and sorrows, at the beginning of the *Canon ;* meditate on His Crucifixion at the *Elevation ;* on His agony on the Cross, at the *Agnus Dei,* or "*Lamb of God, who takest away the sins of the world ;*" on His Burial, at the Communion; on His Resurrection, at the Post Communion; on His Ascension, at the *Ite Missa est ;* and at the blessing meditate on the last benediction given by this dear Redeemer to His Blessed Mother, Apostles and Disciples, when He was ascending into Heaven. These considerations may be accompanied with sighs and tears and other sentiments of love and tenderness for your dear Saviour.

In meditating on these mysteries, you may, if so disposed, say vocal prayers, which should be united with those of Jesus Christ and of the priest. Be very careful to keep these mysteries of the Incarnation, Life, Sufferings, Passion, Death, Resurrection, and Ascension of Christ in your heart.

In the course of these meditations, remember to pray for the living, before the Elevation, and for the dead after the Elevation; and to make a spiritual communion, at the time the priest receives the Communion. This spiritual communion consists in an ardent desire of receiving sacramentally, were it permitted, the most holy Sacrament. Endeavour to purify your soul by an act of perfect contrition, and conceive a most profound sentiment of humility, similar to that of the centurion who exclaimed, *"Lord I am not worthy that Thou shouldst enter into my house ; but only say the word, and Thy servant shall be healed."*

After Mass, you may say—

"I most humbly ask pardon, O my God. for all my distractions and irreverences; and return Thee infinite thanks for Thy bounty in allowing me to assist at this august Sacrifice; bestow Thy blessings on me, I beseech

Thee, that during the remainder of the day I may preserve the remembrance and love of Jesus Christ. Amen."

CHAPTER V.

OF WORK AND SILENCE.

At the beginning of your work, offer it up with a most pure intention of the glory of God, performing it through obedience, looking for nothing but His most holy will, which is manifested by your Rules and your Superiors. Perform it leisurely, and without hurry, lest you might injure your health. At the same time you should do it well and with diligence. Raise your heart from time to time, to God; and be on your guard, lest vanity or self-complacency rob you of the merit of your good actions.

After your work, return thanks to God for the assistance He has been pleased to give you, and give glory to Him for whatever may seem deserving of praise.

When you work in company with others, let your discourse be worthy of a religious; and in hours of silence, observe it with inviolable exactness. That your observance of the rule of silence may be meritorious, propose to yourself the following intentions:— Observe holy silence in obedience to your rules, to honor and imitate the silence of Jesus Christ in the sacred womb of His

Mother, for the space of nine months, or during the time of His infancy, or during the forty days passed in the desert, or the three days He remained in the tomb; or let it be observed in punishment of so many criminal and useless words said by you during your life. You should particularly bear in mind that silence is commanded; that by suspending all intercourse with others, you may have a more easy means of sweet interior conversation with God. Hence in time of silence let your mind and heart be engaged with God.

CHAPTER VI.

OF MEALS.

Before meals, be careful to offer this action to God, and not to engage therein but through obedience and through a motive of His pure love, suffer not sensuality to steal on you.

Go to table, reflecting on the extreme frugality of Jesus, Mary and Joseph, and having also in mind the necessities of the poor who have not wherewith to satisfy their hunger. These thoughts will suggest to you many holy affections.

Assist at the blessing of the table with modesty and attention, and long after the food of angels, the feast of eternity, of which God shall be our Provider, our Food, our All. O happy Eternity! when wilt thou come?

During the meal—first keep strict silence; secondly, observe decorum and sobriety in eating; thirdly, taste God in all that is sweet; remember the Passion of Jesus Christ in what is disagreeable and palatable; fourthly, do not omit the sacrifice of some small morsel of what is most agreeable to you; finally, attend to the reading at table, and gather some sentiment for your soul to feast on.

Having returned thanks with respect and attention, be foremost to lend assistance in the kitchen in all that is humble, and devote to God's service the strength you have received by eating, forming a determination of devoting it to His glory and pure love.

CHAPTER VII.

OF RECREATION.

Offer your recreation to God before commencing it, with a resolution of doing or saying nothing which may offend God, or hurt Christian charity.

Bear in mind the sweet and amiable recreations of Jesus, Mary and Joseph, and make yours similar to theirs.

Ask of God the grace of diverting yourself well; I say so; for it is necessary both for soul as well as body, in order to be able to persevere in the service of God; but it should be done w   ·   ce of manner, and according to the rules of religious decorum.

In recreation be as gay, amiable, frank and cordial as you can, avoid all sadness and melancholy, do not single out one Sister for an associate, as particular friendships are schisms in communities, do not yield to immoderate fits of loud laughter, or boisterous talk, avoid, as a pest, all marks of coldness or aversion, uncharitable words, bitter offensive raillery, in a word, anything that might in ever so slight a degree, wound charity, or the decorum of a house consecrated to God.

Practise in your recreation the laudable custom of many religious houses, where a Sister is appointed to correct any departure from decorum, and to remind occasionally, the assembly of the presence of God. Let the same be adopted for the preservation of modesty in your recreation. Endeavor to draw some subject of conversation from the lecture read at table, or from some such matter, without, however, forcing the mind, but with sweet gaiety and innocent mirth, and so as to promote both recreation and devotion at the same time.

After recreation, ask pardon of God for any faults you may have committed during it, and place yourself again in the Divine Presence.

CHAPTER VIII.

OF THE MORNING AND EVENING EXAMINATION OF CONSCIENCE.

There are two kinds of examination of conscience—the particular and the general. The particular examination consists in applying the mind to examine some particular fault or sin, to which one is more subject. A person makes some reflection on this particular subject every day, and searches for the remedy to be employed until the fault is corrected; some slight penance should be self-imposed. This particular examination may also be employed as an aid in acquiring any particular virtue, of which we may stand in need, by examining whether we advance or lose ground in the practise of the particular virtue; by resolving to practise this same virtue so many times a day, and performing some penance when one has failed. This particular examination is most necessary in order to correct our defects and to advance in virtue.

The general examination is made of the sins committed, either since arriving at the use of reason, or since the last confession, or since the last examination. As the general examination is commanded by the Constitutions to be made twice a-day, the Sisters shall make it in the following manner:—

Having knelt down and adored God, consider yourself as a poor criminal in His sight, who desires to find out your faults, and obtain pardon of them. Address him in these words:—

"My God, I thank Thee with my whole heart for all the graces I have received from Thy bounty.

"Grant me, O my God, the light necessary for me in order to know my sins, and grace to repent of them with my whole heart."

Let your mind be occupied in considering your conduct and considering your sins. Make this examination with exactness, and quickly; afterwards, make acts of contrition. You may say:—

"My God, I beg pardon, from the bottom of my heart, for all the sins I have committed against Thy Divine Will. I detest them, and am sorry for them, not only because by my sins I have deserved the rigor of Thy chastisements, but still more because by them I have offended Thee, O Infinite Bounty. whom I ought to love, and whom I now love above all things. I now resolve, through Thy grace, rather to die than ever again to offend Thee for the time to come, and to do penance for my sins even unto death."

In your examination every morning and evening, take a review of those faults you more frequently fall into; resolve on correcting yourself by adopting the most effectual means for that purpose.

CHAPTER IX.

ON GOING TO BED.

After the examination of conscience, perform the lecture and say the prayers which are prescribed in Chapter V. of Part V., of these Constitutions. You shall then observe what is here laid down:

Be quick in undressing; observe the greatest modesty, so that neither you, nor any one who might be in the room, can see you at all uncovered. In undressing yourself, beg of God that you may entirely lay aside the old, and put on the new man—namely, the virtues of Jesus Christ.

Lie down in that posture in which you would do, if Jesus Christ were present; remember, when in bed, that this Divine Saviour and several Saints used to sleep on the bare floor, and that, in a short time, your body will be in the cold grave.

Offer your sleep to the Almighty: unite it with that of Jesus Christ, when on earth: beg of the Glorious Virgin, St. Joseph, all the Angels and Saints, and especially your Guardian Angel, to adore, love, and pray to God for you, whilst you sleep. Finally take your cross with humility and love, saying as Jesus Christ said—"Father, into Thy hands I commend my spirit." Leave your cross on your heart; fold your arms into the form of a cross, and say—"Jesus, Mary and Joseph;" and try always to have some good thought in your mind before falling asleep.

PART II.

Of the Exercises of the Week

CHAPTER I.

OF THE MANNER OF SANCTIFYING ALL THE DAYS OF THE WEEK.

Consecrate Sunday to the most Holy, Adorable Trinity; and practise on this day acts of self-annihilation in the Divine Presence, of zeal, of desire of making this ineffable mystery known, loved and adored by the whole world.

Offer up, with this view, all the actions of the day.

Let Monday be devoted to the suffrage of the souls of the faithful departed, for whose spiritual consolation you will offer up all the actions of the day.

Tuesday may be allotted to the devotion of the holy Angels, but particulary of your Guardian Angel. Imitate them, by leading a life altogether detached from the world, and intimately united with God: honor, love and thank them for their excessive charity in attending on and serving you at all times.

Let Wednesday be employed in honoring the Holy Ghost by inflamed sentiments of love for your Divine Spouse, for Jesus, as also for your neighbor.

Thursday is specially consecrated to the most adorable Sacrament of the altar. Practise, during this day, acts of love, faith, devotion and adoration towards your amiable Saviour in this most wonderful Sacrament. Often express your deep sorrow for all the contempt and outrages which He receives in this mystery of His love. Imitate Him in His entire annihilation of Himself here, by a most profound humilation of yourself.

Friday should be passed in devotion to the Passion of this dear Redeemer. Endeavor to excite in yourself, through love for Him, the anguish He felt in sufferings and death.

Saturday is devoted to the Glorious Mother. Conceive, in her honor, an ardent desire of imitating her modesty and meekness. Commemorate, also, on this day, the glory of your holy Patriarch, St. Joseph, and the triumphs of the Saints, resolving to aspire with renewed efforts to the perfection of your state.

The Sisters might, also, with the approbation of the Superior, if there be time, form Conferences of Virtue among themselves, on the following points :—

If you have united in spirit your hearts, offering them in the most perfect union of love to the most Holy Trinity, placing them at the foot of the Cross, or in the Wounds of Jesus, or at the feet of Mary;

If you have corrected a certain fault, as curiosity, loud speaking, hastiness of temper, or the like;

If you have practised any virtuous action previously prescribed, giving also an account, with great candor and humility, of the manner of discharging the pious exercises or sentiments of devotion with which God inspired you.

You might at the commencement of these Conferences, recite the *Veni Creator*, to invoke the Holy Spirit, and at the end of them say the *Litany* of the Blessed Virgin.

CHAPTER II.

OF CONFESSION.

When about to prepare for Confession, kneel down, recite the hymn of the holy Ghost, *Veni Creator ;* and ask the grace of performing well this action, which is one of the most important for our salvation.

Then examine your conscience as mentioned above; and prepare yourself for each confession as you would wish to do it were you preparing for death.

You can thus order your sins: first placing

those again God: then those against your Superior, your neighbor and yourself, mentioning briefly in what you may have offended God by thought, words, deeds, or omissions. If this arrangement embarrass you adopt whatever method may be most convenient. Avoid, in confession, long details: confess the sin in as few words as possible, not omitting such circumstances as are necessary; in nothing excusing yourself, except as far as is required to make known how far you are guilty, not accusing others; never mentioning the names of others. Do not go to confession through custom, vanity, human respect, through scrupulosity, or inconsiderately; but with humility and simplicity, with sorrow and confusion, declare your sins at the feet of the minister of Jesus Christ, in order to obtain the pardon of them.

Appear before the priest, as Magdalen at the feet of Jesus; ask his blessing, and say the *Confiteor* to the words *mea culpa*. Then accuse yourself of your sins, remembering that it is to Jesus Christ you confess, for the priest possesses His power and authority.

Having confessed your sins, you may, with great advantage to your soul, and according to the advice of St. Francis de Sales, accuse yourself of some sin of your past life already confessed, in order to renew in your heart the sorrow for your past sins, and that there may be certain matter for the priest's absolution. You shall terminate in these words: "Of these sins, and of all others to me unknown, I most humbly ask pardon, O my God, and of you, Father, penance and absolution." Then finish the *Confiteor*; renew your act of contrition, whilst the priest pronounces absolution.

Receive with humility the penance imposed on you, and listen to the advice of the Confessor as coming from Jesus Christ; bear it in your mind, and have a great desire of profiting by it. If the Confessor were to advise anything contrary to the customs of your house, or impose a penance you could not perform, you will respectfully excuse yourself.

After absolution, rise up with a deep sense of gratitude to God, who has pardoned you through His minister.

After confession, do not forget to make your acts of thanksgiving, and most particularly renew your resolutions of amending your faults, and of keeping the promises made to God in confession. Retain the sentiments of contrition as long as you can, and perform the penance imposed on you as soon as you can, and with great devotion. Speak not of your confession, **and never mention your penance.**

CHAPTER III.

OF HOLY COMMUNION.

This Sacrament requires such great preparation, that it ought to make us tremble. So great, however, is the bounty of Jesus Christ, that He is satisfied provided we approach Him with ardent love, profound humility, and purity of heart.

On the eve of Communion, perform some mortification, or other act, in order to prepare your heart for its Lord. Long for the moment of Communion. At night, fall asleep with this thought, and in the moment of awaking let it be your first reflection. With short and pious ejaculations express your loving desire of possessing Jesus, in your bosom. Ask your Mother, Mary, to pray for you; also your holy Patriarch, St. Joseph, and all the Saints, to pray for you, that your soul may be prepared to receive your God. St. Bernard used to exclaim—" I desire to receive Thee, O my Jesus! a million of times I desire it! Ah! when will You come to dwell within me?"

Direct a good portion of your morning prayer to dispose you for communion. Every other action may be directed to the same end; you may wash your hands and your mouth for this purpose. Avoid all possible occasions, not only of talking, but even of distraction. Preserve yourself in a sweet and loving silence.

Let Mass be heard, if possible, with more than usual fervor; be occupied in purifying your soul by acts of humility, contrition, faith, desire; by considerations of the Infinite Majesty of Jesus, which will impress on the mind great respect, accompanied with sentiments of tender love for your dear Spouse and an ardent wish of receiving Him.

Offer the Communion you are about to make, for the same intentions as you offer up the Sacrifice of the Mass, namely—to glorify God, to thank Him for all His benefits, to obtain pardon of sins, to acquire the graces you stand in need of, and to renew the memory of the Passion and Death of Jesus Christ.

You can unite these general intentions with your special intentions either for yourself, for your Congregation, or Community; your relatives, friends, or enemies, or the general wants of the Church or of the diocese; or for souls of the faithful in Purgatory. You can join all these intentions in one Communion.

Having gently swallowed the sacred Host, retire to your place with great piety, making a reverence to the altar. Endeavor to be all inflamed with love for the God of love whom you possess within you and make the following five acts:—

Adore Him profoundly, and invite all creatures in heaven and on earth to join with you in adoring Him; particularly dedicate for this purpose all the powers of your soul and body.

Thank Him with all your strength for His condescension in coming to lodge within you, and invite all creatures to return Him thanks millions of times for this inestimable favor.

Love Him in return for His infinite love towards you; renounce all things that may displease Him in you; give yourself up to His Holy Will without reserve, by the entire sacrifice of yourself to do what is most pleasing to Him, both in time and eternity. Ask, at this important moment, for those virtues you most need; the correction of those vices and defects which still domineer over you, and by the extirpation of which God may be most glorified. Pray, also, for the necessities of the whole world, of the whole Church, for the heads of it, for this diocese, the congregation, your parents, friends, enemies, those recommended to your prayers, those under your care, and for all the souls in Purgatory. Do not forget to direct your intention to gain the Indulgences which may be gained at the time.

In the fifth place, pray with great fervor that before leaving you He may bestow on you His benediction, and that this benediction may produce in you a change similar to that which is effected by the Consecration, by which as the bread is changed into Himself, you be entirely changed into Him, so that He may live in you; that He may govern your thoughts, passions, desires, inclinations, words, works and intentions, thus fulfilling the very words of Christ—" He that eateth Me, the same also shall live by Me."*

Before you terminate your thanksgiving, offer to Jesus Christ all you are about to do, and all you perform until your next Communion, in thanks for this great mercy shown you. Enter then on your occupations, but, as much as possible, without distracting yourself, or losing sight of the presence of Jesus Christ. Imitate the most Blessed Virgin, who carried in her womb the same Jesus whom you possess. She also bore Him in her mind, in her heart, in her memory; she was influenced in all her actions by Him, by His charity, His patience, humilty, purity—in fine, by all His virtues, so that it was no longer she that lived, but Jesus who lived in her, as St. Paul says of himself.

You should, in like manner, after communion, live no longer, but Jesus should live in you; the life and virtues of your dear Redeemer should be visible in your whole exterior, and God Himself should witness it in your interior.

---

* St. John, 6.

CHAPTER IV.

OF FASTING, DISCIPLINE, AND OTHER PRACTICES OF THE WEEK.

All your works of piety and penitential practices are without merit, if you do not perform them in Jesus Christ, your Head, whose spirit must animate and regulate all you do, that it may be holy and agreeable in the eyes of His Father.

Hence, unite your fasts with the fasts of Jesus Christ; and as He fasted so rigorously as to suffer hunger, do you also fast that your body may suffer according as your health and duties will permit. When you use the discipline, unite it with the scourging which Jesus endured for your sins, and remember that His most Sacred Body was torn and mangled to teach you not to spare yourself.

There are two other weekly exercises— namely, the *Chapter on Faults* and the *Conferences;* but as we have already spoken of the manner in which they are to be conducted, in the sixth and seventh chapters of the sixth part of the Constitutions, we shall say nothing of them in this place.

PART III.

Of the Exercises of each Month.

CHAPTER I.

OF THE PROTESTATIONS.

After the Sisters shall have received communion, as prescribed, on the first day of each month, all being assembled together, shall make in an audible tone of voice the following protestations, in order to renew in their mind the spirit of fervor in the observance of their rules. The Superior, or some other Sister, shall read them aloud, and the others shall at the same time repeat them with humility and devotion, and with a firm intention of reducing them to practice through the means of God's graces.

Protestations.

We, here assembled in the presence of the most Holy and Adorable Trinity, Father, Son and **Holy Ghost**, of the Glorious Virgin Mary, of our Patriarch St. Joseph, and of all the Saints of Heaven, protest most humbly, though entirely distrustful of ourselves, yet confiding in the assistance of the Divine Grace and Infinite Bounty:—

1. To maintain inviolably the closest union of our souls with God, by the exercise of His love and the continual study of His presence, and by the most cordial and perfect charity amongst ourselves, and not to permit nor to do anything, however slight, contrary thereto.

2. To practise everywhere and on all occasions, the most profound humility, but particularly to avoid all offices, and all competition which may be formed for them, whatever may be the pretext or prospect of good presented to us;

3. To aspire always to the practice of what we know to be most perfect in all things. especially in the exact observance of whatever is contained in the spiritual maxims, and in our Constitutions, making account of every matter, however small, and desiring rather to die than to violate any of them;

4. Besides the diligence that each one shall have to keep the rules of her particular office, to unite in such a manner among ourselves, that all that is laid down in our Constitutions respecting the choice of Superiors, the reception, dismissal and education of Sisters, shall be observed **with rigorous exactness;**

5. To avoid as a pestilence all particular attachments, either among ourselves, or with lay persons; as, also, whatever might wound charity; also, not to make known, or to murmur among ourselves, or to speak on any account whatever the faults of the Superior, or of our equals, or of our inferiors, to persons unconnected with the Community, but solely to those who may have it in their power to remedy the evil;

6. Not to speak out of our houses with any person whatsoever, unless it be immediately necessary in the service of the sick poor, and to make known the disorders and necessities of the different districts;

7. In our houses, not to speak with lay persons, except in spiritual matters and concerning their spiritual advancement, and for their relief and consolation in afflictions; and besides, to observe inviolably, both as to the manner and length of those visits, what is laid down in our Constitutions;

8. To live in the profession and practice of such poverty as requires nothing more than barely what is necessary;

9. Affectionately to cherish meekness, humility, and sincerity, and to carefully avoid the least thing contrary to these virtues.

May God, in His goodness, condescend to bestow on us the grace to live and die in the exact observance of these protestations. **Amen.**

CHAPTER II.

THE PATRONS OF EACH MONTH, AND OTHER EXERCISES.

Besides the protestation, the Sisters ought to choose, each month, a Patron Saint; also ought to make an agreement with two or three Sisters to watch one another in the practice of some particular virtue, and correct one another for all the faults committed against this virtue; which is called *Admonition*. At the end of the month, they ought to make a confession of the month; but as we have prescribed all the rules of these practices, in the second chapter of the sixth part of these Constitutions, we refer the Sisters to it. We shall merely recommend strict attention to the practices of the Admonition, and monthly confession, as most important for your spiritual advancement, and the neglect of which cannot fail to be attended with considerable falling off in the way of perfection.

Be on your guard, when you have chosen a Saint for the month, not to say that you are not satisfied, or that you do not love the Saint, or that you would wish to have another; for such sentiments are injurious to God and the Saints; on the contrary you should love and esteem the Saint whom God has given you, and desire no other.

PART IV.

Of the Annual Exercises.

CHAPTER I.

THE MANNER OF BEGINNING THE YEAR.

Prepare yourself for the commencement of the new year by a review and general confession of the past year. Let your meditation for the last day of the year which is about to end, be, on the benefits received, to return infinite thanks for them; on all the sins committed, that you may ask pardon for them; and, thirdly, meditate on, and ask of the Almighty, what He desires of you during the following year, that you may resolve on performing it punctually.

On the first day of the year make your New Year's gift of the Infant Jesus, and ask a return from Him. Observe the same with regard to the Blessed Virgin, St. Joseph and all the Saints for whom you feel most devotion you shall make New Year's gift to them, also in the following manner:

Offer the new year to God, with the most fervent desire of passing it well. That this offering may be made effectual, make use of the intentions laid down in the chapter on the Holy Sacrifice of the Mass;

Offer yourself to God the Father, and declare that, for His honor, you desire to do what you know is most agreeable to Him and what is most perfect, that you may be perfect as your Heavenly Father is perfect.

Offer yourself to God the Son, and protest that, for the love of Him, you desire to annihilate yourself by the practice of the most profound humility, and by dying to all your humors, caprices and vicious inclinations; that thus you may imitate the annihilation He effected of Himself in His Passion for the love of you;

Offer yourself to God the Holy Ghost, and protest that, in all things, you desire to practise the most pure and perfect love of God; and to be all love in religion, as He is the substantial love of the Father and Son;

Offer yourself to the Incarnate Son of God, your Saviour Jesus Christ, burning for the salvation of souls, and protest that, in imitation of Him, you desire to live and labor unceasingly for the salvation of souls, and even to die in their service, as He lived, labored and suffered, without ceasing, for your salvation and others, and even died for the Redemption of the world;

Offer yourself to the ever Blessed Virgin, and make a protestation, in her presence, to imitate her perfect fidelity to Divine grace, and to obey all the movements of the most Adorable Spirit, her Spouse;

Offer yourself to the glorious St. Joseph, and protest, in his presence, to imitate his perfect charity, in respect to every class of neighbors.

At the end of these offerings and protestations you shall ask the Divine blessing, and the grace of fulfilling them.

CHAPTER II.

OF RETREATS, AND OF THE ANNUAL RENOVATION OF VOWS.

In the first chapter of Part VI. of the Constitutions we have prescribed the Annual Confession, the Annual Renovation of Vows, and various retreats, concerning which we do not deem it necessary to give any other rules here; not to increase this Directory, already very considerable, and also because Rodriguez, and other spiritual writers, give rules for such exercises. You can follow the advice of your Superiors, and make choice of the book which they may suggest in performing these exercises.

We conclude by exhorting you to the perfect observance of all your exercises, and of the methods laid down in the Directory, in order to perform them in a holy manner.

Manner of receiving and giving the Habit to the Sisters of St. Joseph.

The Celebrant, kneeling before the altar, shall intone the hymn *Veni Creator Spiritus*, etc. The assistants, or the Sisters shall sing the remainder of it, and then the Celebrant shall say:—

V. Emitte Spiritum tuum, et creabuntur.
R. Et renovabis faciem terræ.

Oremus.

Deus, qui corda fidelium Sancti Spiritus illustratione docuisti, da nobis in eodem Spiritu recta sapere: et de ejus semper consolatione gaudere. Per Christum Dominum, etc.

He shall then bless the habit, placed on the Epistle side of the altar, saying:—

V. Adjutorium nostrum in nomine Domini.
R. Qui fecit cœlum et terram.
V. Dominus vobiscum.
R. Et cum spiritu tuo.

Oremus.

Deus æternorum bonorum fidelissime Promissor, et certissime Persolutor, qui vestimun tum **salutis, et indumentum jucunditatis** æternæ tuis fidelibus promisiti: Clementiam tuam supplices exoramus, ut hoc indumentum (vel hæc indumenta); humilitatem cordis et contemptum mundi significans (vel significantia) quo hæc famula tua est (vel quibus hæc famulæ tuæ sunt), visibiliter informanda (vel informandæ), propitius bene † dicas, et beatæ abnegationis habitum, quem te inspiranta suscipit (vel suscipiunt), te protegente custodiat (vel custodiant), et quam (vel quas) venerandis vestibus Congregationis Sancti Joseph, temporaliter induis, beatæ facias immortalitate vestiri. Per Dominum nostrum, etc.

Here he sprinkles it with holy water; afterwards, being seated on the platform of the altar, he makes an exhortation to the Aspirant, who is kneeling. If the discourse be long, she can sit down. After the discourse, he thus addresses her.

C. What do you ask, my child?

N. I ask for the habit of the Sisters of the Congregation of St. Joseph.

C. Are you fully resolved to wear it with devotion, and to live and die in the exact observance of the rules prescribed for the Sisters who wear this habit?

N. Yes, I am fully resolved on it.

C. In order to become a true Sister of **St. Joseph,** you should, my child, die to the world, to your parents, to your friends, and to yourself, and live alone for **Jesus Christ.**

N. This is what I desire with all my heart: that the world be nothing more for me, and Jesus be my only possession.

C. Do you desire at once to renounce the world, its vanities, and its pomps, and to take the poor habit of the Sisters of St. Joseph?

N. It is a long time that I have ardently desired it, and I beg of you not to defer it any longer.

C. I am satisfied to do so, my child, and wish Mother Superior to receive you into the Congregation, to retrench this superfluity of hair, and divest you of the vanity of your worldly dress, in order to put on the poor habit you long for with such ardor, and at the same time to clothe you with Jesus Christ. Go then, my child, to receive this holy habit.

(The aspirant shall go out to put on the habit, and at the same time the Celebrant sings or recites the psalm, *In exitu Israel de Ægypto,* and also the psalms, *Lætatus sum in his quæ dicta sunt mihi,* and *Laudate pueri Dominum,* if necessary.)

When the Novice returns, the Celebrant says to her—

C. Behold, now you are dead to the world, my child, are you satisfied?

N. Yes, I am quite satisfied: I experience the most perfect joy of heart.

C. You have reason to be satisfied, as at this moment, by a special favor of God, you begin to have, in a most particular manner, St. Joseph for your father, the most Blessed Virgin for your Mother, and Jesus Christ for your Spouse.

N. I value this favor above all the goods of the world. These glorious advantages enable me to leave with joy my parents, my friends, and the vanities of the world. And I implore of God the grace of persevering unto death in the profession of the life of the poor Sisters of St. Joseph, which I have so long desired, and which I on this day commence to embrace, in having received their holy habit.

The Celebrant gives her the name she desires, and then blesses her saying—

C. May God be praised, Sister, for the good sentiments which He gives you; and I beg He may accompany them with His gracious benedictions. In the Name of the Father, and of the Son, and of the Holy Ghost. Amen.

The Celebrant sings the Te Deum Laudamus with the choir; and being ended, he retires. The Superior and Sisters, one after another, salute and embrace the Novice, and conduct her into the house.

The Manner of Receiving the Profession of the Sisters of the Congregation of St. Joseph.

The Novice kneeling before the Altar, with the Superior and Assistant at her sides, the

Celebrant addresses a short exhortation to her, at the end of which he interrogates her as follows:—

C. What do you ask for, my child?

N. I beg, for the love of God, to make my profession, and to be received into the Congregation of St. Joseph, in order to devote my whole life to the service of God and of my neighbor.

C. Have you, my child, seriously thought on the obligations you contract in making your profession in this Congregation?

N. I have most seriously reflected on it; and having an experience of it during my novitiate, I hope with the grace of God, to comply with its obligations, as far as my weakness will allow.

C. Have you quite freely, willingly, and purely for the love of God, resolved to take the three simple vows of poverty, chastity and obedience, and faithfully to keep them?

N. It is, with all my heart, with my free will and from the sole love of God, that I have resolved to renounce altogether myself entirely, to leave the riches, pleasures, honors, and all creatures, in order to make profession of the poverty, chastity and obedience of Jesus Christ, whom alone I wish to love, faithfully to imitate all my life; and in order to satisfy the pressing desire which the Holy Spirit gives me, I most humbly supplicate you to receive immediately the vows which I am going to make to God.

The Celebrant addressing the Superior and Sisters, says to them—

C. You have heard, Sisters, the pressing request, which this Novice has made. Do you give your consent on the part of the Congregation?

The Superior replies—

S. Yes: our Sisters wish that, by the grace of God, she may have the happiness of living and dying with them in the Congregation, and that she now take the holy vows, and make her holy profession according to the form of our Institute.

The Celebrant says to the Novice—

C. Courage, then, my child; if such be your wish, come and offer your vows to God, your Creator, and you shall be instructed by His Divine light and inflamed by His most pure love.

The Novice pronounces her vows, saying with profound respect, great attention, and sincere intention—

N. My God, All powerful and Eternal Being, I, N. N., thy most unworthy daughter and servant, desirous of living exclusively for Thee, and of being subject to Thy grace—in the presence of Jesus Christ, Thy Eternal Son, and of His Glorious Virgin Mother Mary, of our Holy Patriarch St. Joseph, and of the whole Court of Heaven, make to

Thy Divine Majesty the vows of perpetual poverty, chastity and obedience, in the Congregation of the Sisters of St. Joseph; and before you, Reverend Father—who hold the place of our Archbishop (or Bishop), our most reverend Superior; and I promise, according to the rules of the said Congregation, to practise, through the grace of God, the most profound humility in all things, and the most cordial charity toward my neighbor, whom I desire to serve by the exercise of all the works of mercy, both spiritual and corporal, required by our Institute. Receive, my God, this offering in the odor of sanctity. Amen.

If the Bishop celebrate, the Novice shall say —"*And in your hands, Right Reverend Father.*"

If before an Archbishop, —"*Most Reverend Father.*"

The Celebrant shall rise and say the following prayer:—

V. Dominus vobiscum.
R. Et cum spiritu tuo.

Oremus.

Omnipotens sempiterne Deus, qui humanæ fragilitatis infirmitatem agnoscis, respice, quæsumus, super hanc famulam tuam (vel hac famulas tuas), et larga tuæ bene † dictionis abundantia imbecillatem ejus (vel earum) corrobora: ut promissa nunc vota, quæ præveniendo aspirasti per auxilium gratiæ tuæ

sancte et religiose a vivendo, valeat (vel valeant) vigilanter observare, et observando ad vitam pervenire sempiternam. Per Christum Dominum nostrum. Amen.

Then the Celebrant blesses the Cross.

V. Adjutorum nostrum in nomine Domini.
R. Qui fecit cœlum et terram.
V. Dominus vobiscum.
R. Et cum spiritu tuo.

Oremus:

Rogamus te, Domine Sancte, Pater Omnipotens, Æterne Deus, ut digneris benedicere † signum Crucis, ut sit remedium salutare generi humano, sit soliditas fidei, profectus bonorum operum, redemptio animarum: sit solamen et protectio, ac tutela contra sæva jacula inimicorum. Per Dominum nostrum Jesum Christum. Amen.

The Celebrant gives the Cross to the Novice, saying—

Receive, my child, the Cross of our Lord Jesus Christ, to which you are affixed with Him by the three vows, as by so many nails: wear it openly on your breast, as a most sure defence against all the attacks of the enemy: and especially endeavor to carry it faithfully in your heart by loving it tenderly, and by bearing with delight and humility this sweet burden: that faithfully living and dying in the love of the Cross with Jesus, you may also triumph with Him in glory

He then says the following prayer and blesses the Professed Sister:—

Oremus.

Respice, quæsumus, Domine, super hanc famulam tuam pro qua (vel hac famulas tuas pro quibus) Dominus noster Jesus Christus non dubitavit manibus tradi nocentium, et crucis subiri tormentum, Qui tecum vivit et regnat.

Benedictio Dei Patris Omnipotentis, Patris, et Filii, et Spiritus Sancti descendant super te (vel vos) et maneat semper.

Then the Te Deum Laudamus *is sung, and the Superior and Sisters salute the newly Professed.*

FORM OF THE ACT TO BE WRITTEN ON THE RECEPTION OF SISTERS.

We, Superior and Sisters of the Congregation of St. Joseph, of the house of N. N., assembled in Chapter, having examined, or caused to be examined, N. N., born in N. N., and aged N. years, have admitted her to receive our holy habit, which, by the permission of our Superiors, has been given to her (or we have given it to her), with the name of Sister N. N., the N. day of the month of N., in the year of our Lord N. N.

In testimony of which we have subscribed this present act.

FORM OF THE ACT TO BE WRITTEN FOR A PROFESSION.

I, Sister N., lawful daughter of N. N., born in the parish of N.; county of N., State of N., aged N., declare and certify, that, by the grace of God, I have received the habit of the Congregation of the Sisters of St. Joseph, in our house of N., the N. day of the month of N., in the year of our Lord N.; and afterwards I made my novitiate in the said house of N., during the space of N.; in which time, having practised the exercises and observed the rules of the said Congregation, I have on this N. day of the month of N., in the year N., voluntarily and freely made my profession, in the hands of N. N., in the church or chapel of N., taking the simple vows of perpetual poverty, chastity and obedience, in the said Congregation, according to its Rules and Constitutions, in presence of N. and N.

In testimony of which I have signed this present act, on the same day.

N. N.

Letter of the Bishop Henry de Maupas, of Puy, for the Establishment of the Sisters of St. Joseph.

We, HENRY DE MAUPAS-DU-TOUR, Bishop of Puy, Count de Velay, immediate Suffragan of the Right Reverend Abbot of St.

Denis of Rheims, Counsellor of the King, and First Almoner of the Queen-Regent, being desirous of advancing the glory of God, the salvation of souls, and the exercise of charity in our diocese, and having heard that certain pious females are anxious to consecrate themselves to works of charity, as well for the hospital and the sick of our city, as also for the education and direction of the orphans of Montferrand; and that, in order to devote themselves the better to said duties, they desire, with our good will and consent, to form a Society and Congregation, in which living in Community, they may be more at leisure, without impediment, to be occupied in said services. This design has appeared to us so laudable, that we have most gladly embraced it, and we have permitted and permit the said females to organize a Congregation under the name and the title of the "SISTERS OF ST. JOSEPH," to assemble and live in community, in one or in several houses, as it may be required, to diffuse more widely the fruit of their charity, and to augment the number of their houses in all the places of our diocese as we may judge proper. Finally, that all things may be done in due order, and that this Congregation may prosper, we have drawn up and given to the said pious persons, rules, which they are to observe with great exactness, for the greater glory of God, and for the edifi-

ation of their neighbor, as they have commenced to do at the afore-mentioned Hospital of Montferrand. Taking these pious persons and their Congregations at present existing, and those to be formed in future, under our protection, we order our Vicars-General and Officials to advance this laudable enterprise, and to watch lest any should be found to molest them ; to whom we give our benediction in all the extent of our most sincere affection, and invoke on them with the same affection the benediction of the Father, and of the Son, and of the Holy Ghost. Amen.

Given at Puy, tenth day of May, One Thousand Six Hundred and Fifty-one (1651).

† HENRY,
Bishop of Puy,
Count of Velay,
L * * * * * *

(*By Order.*)

GIRARDIN, *Secretary.*

Alla Santità di Nostro Signore, Pio P. P. IX.
felicemente regnante:

I sottoscritti Oratori della Santità Vostra, Giovanni Vescovo di Buffalo, Giovanni Vescovo di Brooklyn, Giacomo Federico Vescovo Filadelfia, Giovanni Vescovo di Hamilton, Giovanni Vescovo di Toronto, nell' America del Nord, hanno nelle loro rispettive Diocesi le Comunità della Suore di San Guiseppe, ammontando presentemente il loro numero circa a 250 persone, istituite originalmente dal Vescovo Enrico de Maupas nella città di Puy in Velay nella Francia, nell' anno 1620, viventi sotto una regola edificante ed approvata da Francesco Paolo de Neuville de Villeroy Arcivescovo e Conte di Lione e Primate di Francia nel 1729. Queste pie suore si occupano in tutte le buone opere prescritte dalle loro Costituzioni, e sono state e sono una sorgente di gran bene ai fedeli, e di consolazione ai loro rispettivi Vescovo, i quali si fanno ora a pregare la Santità Vostra di voler concedere a questa disinteressate e divote Religiose, in qaulunque modo lo stimerà la prudenza e la Carità della Santità Vostra, un segno della Paterna Vostra approvazione onde vieppiu.

incoraggiarle nel disempegno dei doveri prescritti dalle loro Regole, e collegarle sempre più nell' affezione e nell' obbedienza alla Santa Sede Apostolica.

Gli umili Oratori in addizione a qualunque grazia spirituale, che Vostra Santità si compiacerà di concedera alle medesime, suggerirebbero una Indulgenza Plenaria da gaudagnarsi ogni anno dalle dette Suore adempiute le consuete condizioni, nel giorno della Festa di Santa Teresa, e dell' anniversario della loro istituzione per il Vescovo di Maupas, non che l'Apostolica Benedizione da impartirsi loro dai rispettivi Vescovi nel loro ritorno da questa gloriosa Solennità della Canonizzazione dei Martiri del Giappone nella prima visita che faranno alle respettive Comunità stabilite nelle loro Diocesi. Che, etc.

Ex audientia SSmi habita die XV^a., Junii, 1862.

SSmus Dmus noster Pius, Divina Providenta P. P. Nonus (IX.) referente me infrascripto Sacrae Congregationis de Propaganda Fide Secretario benigne annuit pro gratia juxta preces, addita conditione orandi juxta intentionem Summi Pontificis, excepta Indulgentia Plenaria in anniversario fundationis instituti, cui Sanctitas sua subrogare dignata est ad dictam Indulgentiam consequendam, servatis tamen consuetis conditionibus, diem anniversariam religiosae professionis. Contrariis, etc., non obstantibus.

Datum Romae ex aedibus dictae Sacrae Congregationis die et anno praedictis. Gratis sine ulla solutione quovis titulo.

H. CAPALTI,
Secretarius

Pro authentico.
  Jacobus Fredericus,
    Episcopus Philadelphiensis,
      In die Festo Assumptionis, B. M., V.
          A. D. 1862.

These documents are the original Memorial presented to the Holy Father on the occasion of the Canonization of the Japanese martyrs, in June, 1862, and the response of the Holy Father to the same, granting, on the usual conditions, a plenary indulgence to the Sisters of St. Joseph, every year, on the Feast of St. Teresa, and on the anniversary of their religious profession.

www.ingramcontent.com/pod-product-compliance
Lightning Source LLC
Chambersburg PA
CBHW021811230426
43669CB00008B/713